my revision notes

Edexcel AS/A-level Year 1

ECONOMICS A

Quintin Brewer

**HODDER
EDUCATION**
AN HACHETTE UK COMPANY

Hachette UK's policy is to use papers that are natural, renewable and recyclable products and made from wood grown in sustainable forests. The logging and manufacturing processes are expected to conform to the environmental regulations of the country of origin.

Orders: please contact Bookpoint Ltd, 130 Milton Park, Abingdon, Oxon OX14 4SB. Telephone: (44) 01235 827720. Fax: (44) 01235 400454. Email education@bookpoint. co.uk

Lines are open from 9 a.m. to 5 p.m., Monday to Saturday, with a 24-hour message answering service. You can also order through our website: www.hoddereducation.co.uk

ISBN: 978-1-4718-4198-9

© Quintin Brewer and Rachel Cole 2015

First published in 2015 by

Hodder Education,
An Hachette UK Company
Carmelite House
50 Victoria Embankment
London EC4Y 0DZ

www.hoddereducation.co.uk

Impression number   10   9   8   7   6   5   4   3   2   1
Year   2019   2018   2017   2016   2015

Cover photo reproduced by permission of 3dmentat/Fotolia

Illustrations by Integra Software Services Pvt. Ltd, Pondicherry, India

Typeset in Bembo Std Regular 11/13 by Integra Software Services Pvt. Ltd, Pondicherry, India

Printed in Spain

A catalogue record for this title is available from the British Library.

Get the most from this book

Everyone has to decide his or her own revision strategy, but it is essential to review your work, learn it and test your understanding. These Revision Notes will help you to do that in a planned way, topic by topic. Use this book as the cornerstone of your revision and don't hesitate to write in it — personalise your notes and check your progress by ticking off each section as you revise.

Tick to track your progress

Use the revision planner on pages 4 and 5 to plan your revision, topic by topic. Tick each box when you have:

- revised and understood a topic
- tested yourself
- practised the exam questions and gone online to check your answers and complete the quick quizzes

You can also keep track of your revision by ticking off each topic heading in the book. You may find it helpful to add your own notes as you work through each topic.

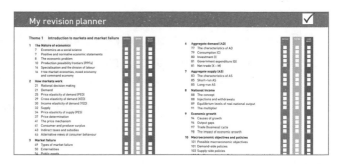

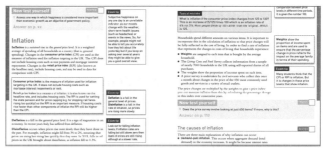

Features to help you succeed

Examiners' tips and summaries

Expert tips are given throughout the book to help you polish your exam technique in order to maximise your chances in the exam. The summaries provide a quick-check bullet list for each topic.

Typical mistakes

The author identifies the typical mistakes candidates make and explains how you can avoid them.

Now test yourself

These short, knowledge-based questions provide the first step in testing your learning. Answers are at the back of the book.

Definitions and key words

Clear, concise definitions of essential key terms are provided where they first appear.

Key words from the specification are highlighted in bold throughout the book.

Revision activities

These activities will help you to understand each topic in an interactive way.

Exam practice

Practice exam questions are provided for each topic. Use them to consolidate your revision and practise your exam skills.

Online

Go online to check your answers to the exam questions and try out the extra quick quizzes at **www.hoddereducation.co.uk/myrevisionnotes**

My revision planner

REVISED   TESTED   EXAM READY

**Exam practice answers and quick quizzes at
www.hoddereducation.co.uk/myrevisionnotes**

Countdown to my exams

- Start by looking at the specification — make sure you know exactly what material you need to revise and the style of the examination. Use the revision planner on pages 4 and 5 to familiarise yourself with the topics.
- Organise your notes, making sure you have covered everything on the specification. The revision planner will help you to group your notes into topics.
- Work out a realistic revision plan that will allow you time for relaxation. Set aside days and times for all the subjects that you need to study, and stick to your timetable.
- Set yourself sensible targets. Break your revision down into focused sessions of around 40 minutes, divided by breaks. These Revision Notes organise the basic facts into short, memorable sections to make revising easier.

REVISED ☐

2–6 weeks to go

- Read through the relevant sections of this book and refer to the examiners' tips, examiners' summaries, typical mistakes and key terms. Tick off the topics as you feel confident about them. Highlight those topics you find difficult and look at them again in detail.
- Test your understanding of each topic by working through the 'Now test yourself' questions in the book. Look up the answers at the back of the book.
- Make a note of any problem areas as you revise, and ask your teacher to go over these in class.
- Look at past papers. They are one of the best ways to revise and practise your exam skills. Write or prepare planned answers to the exam practice questions provided in this book. Check your answers online and try out the extra quick quizzes at **www.hoddereducation.co.uk/ myrevisionnotes**
- Use the revision activities to try out different revision methods. For example, you can make notes using mind maps, spider diagrams or flash cards.
- Track your progress using the revision planner and give yourself a reward when you have achieved your target.

REVISED ☐

One week to go

- Try to fit in at least one more timed practice of an entire past paper and seek feedback from your teacher, comparing your work closely with the mark scheme.
- Check the revision planner to make sure you haven't missed out any topics. Brush up on any areas of difficulty by talking them over with a friend or getting help from your teacher.
- Attend any revision classes put on by your teacher. Remember, he or she is an expert at preparing people for examinations.

REVISED ☐

The day before the examination

- Flick through these Revision Notes for useful reminders, for example the examiners' tips, examiners' summaries, typical mistakes and key terms.
- Check the time and place of your examination.
- Make sure you have everything you need — extra pens and pencils, tissues, a watch, bottled water, sweets.
- Allow some time to relax and have an early night to ensure you are fresh and alert for the examinations.

REVISED ☐

My exams

AS Economics Paper 1

Date:...

Time: ....

Location: ....

AS Economics Paper 2

Date:...

Time: ....

Location: ....

1 The nature of economics

Economics as a social science

Thinking like an economist

Economics is concerned with the ways by which societies organise scarce productive resources in order to satisfy people's wants. It provides a unique and special way of examining many areas of human behaviour which involves using the economist's toolkit of concepts, theories and techniques to analyse economic issues and problems.

Economists often use models to develop theories of behaviour. These models are usually based on assumptions from which certain deductions may be made.

The use of the ceteris paribus assumption in building models

When building models economists work on the basis that all other variables are held constant to enable deductions to be made. This is called the **'ceteris paribus'** assumption which means 'other things being equal'. This helps to simplify analysis so that the impact of a single change in a variable can be examined.

> **Ceteris paribus** means that when the effect of a change in one variable is considered, it is assumed that all other variables are held constant.

The inability in economics to make scientific experiments

It is impossible for economists to conduct laboratory experiments because economics is a social science involving people. Consequently, economic policies which may have been effective at one time in one country may not have the same impact at another time or in another country.

> **Exam tip**
>
> Analysis is usually based on the ceteris paribus assumption. However, in making an evaluative comment, you may find it helpful to remove this assumption.

Positive and normative economic statements

Positive economics

Positive economic statements are based on facts that can be proved or disproved. They include what was, is or will be, and these statements can be verified as being true or false by reference to the date or by using a scientific approach.

As noted above, economists often use models as a way of predicting behaviour. It is possible to make positive statements on the basis of models, such as the impact on price of a product following an increase in demand.

Positive economic statements may be based on official data such as gross domestic product (GDP), prices of commodities, the rate of unemployment, and the exchange rate of one currency against another.

> **Positive economic statements** are objective statements based on evidence or facts which can, therefore, be proved or disproved.

Normative economics

REVISED

Normative economic statements are based on value judgements and are, therefore, subjective. They relate to what:

- might be good or bad, or
- should be or ought to be, or
- would be fair or unfair

Normative economics is usually associated with discussions about economic policy. In this unit, for example, it is concerned with issues such as whether or not there should be:

- a minimum price for alcohol
- subsidies for green energy, e.g. wind farms
- road tolls
- an increase in the tax on cigarettes
- more private sector provision in the health service
- the introduction of a tax on sugary drinks

> **Normative economic** statements are subjective statements based on value judgements and cannot be proved or disproved.

> **Typical mistake**
>
> Answers relating to normative statements often consider them to be opinions. Although this is not technically incorrect, it is much better to use the terms 'value judgements' or 'subjective views' to describe them.

Now test yourself

TESTED

1 Which of the following are positive statements and which are normative statements?
  (a) Taxes on bankers should be increased.
  (b) The GDP of Greece fell by over 25% between 2008 and 2014.
  (c) New technology has caused a fall in the price of mobile phones.
  (d) High energy prices are unfair on the poor.
  (e) Inequality is increasing in the UK.

Answers on p. 108

The economic problem

The problem of scarcity

REVISED

All societies face the problem that wants are infinite but resources are limited in supply. This is the underlying reason for the fundamental economic problem of scarcity. Therefore, choices must be made. The issue of **scarcity** means that societies face a series of questions:

> **Scarcity** exists because resources are finite whereas wants are infinite.

- **What to produce and how much to produce?** This relates to the different types of goods and services the economy should produce and how much of each.

- **How should the goods and services be produced?** Production may be labour intensive, i.e. a high proportion of labour used relative to capital, or capital intensive, i.e. a high proportion of capital used relative to labour.
- **How should the goods produced be allocated?** This is concerned with the distribution of the goods produced and will affect the degree of equality in the society.

Resources

REVISED

The resources of a country are referred to as **'factors of production'**. Four factors of production may be identified:

- **Land:** includes all natural resources, raw materials, the fertility of the soil and resources found in the sea.
- **Labour**: refers to those involved in the production of goods and services and includes all human effort both physical and mental.
- **Capital**: any man-made aid to production including factory buildings, offices, machinery, IT equipment which are used to make other goods and services.
- **Enterprise:** the entrepreneur performs two essential functions:
  - bringing together the other factors of production so that goods and services can be produced and
  - taking the risks involved in production.

> **Factors of production** are resources and include land, labour, capital and enterprise.

> **Typical mistake**
>
> Describing money as capital should be avoided. As a factor of production, capital is something tangible which is used to make other goods.

The distinction between renewable and non-renewable resources

REVISED

Some resources are renewable, i.e. they can be replaced naturally after use, e.g. solar energy, wind power, wood and fish. Such resources are likely to be sustainable unless they are consumed more quickly than they can be replaced. Other resources are non-renewable, i.e. continued consumption will eventually result in their exhaustion. Examples include oil, platinum and copper.

> **Renewable resources** are those whose stock levels can be maintained at a certain level.
>
> **Non-renewable resources** are those which will eventually be completely depleted.

The importance of opportunity costs to economic agents

REVISED

Scarcity implies that choices must be made. However, each choice involves an opportunity cost. This may be explained as follows: If a country's resources are used to manufacture one product, then it must forgo an alternative product that could have been produced. The next best alternative foregone is called the opportunity cost of what has been produced. Opportunity cost, therefore, is a **real cost** measured in terms of something that is foregone.

> **Opportunity cost** is the next best alternative that is forgone when a choice is made.

Examples of opportunity cost include:

- For a consumer: a woman might have enough money to buy either an ebook or an itune. If she decides to buy the ebook then the opportunity cost is the itune.
- For a firm: it might have to make a choice between its two priorities — buying a new IT system and building a new factory. If it chooses the IT system then the opportunity cost is the new factory.

- For the government: suppose it has £10 million with which to fund one of its two main priorities, both requiring a £10 million investment — building a new hospital or building a new university. If it decides that its first preference is the hospital while the second preference is the university, then the opportunity cost of building the hospital will be the university building.

Typical mistake

Considering opportunity cost in terms of money. This is incorrect: opportunity cost must be measured as a real cost, i.e. in terms of goods forgone when a choice is made.

Economic goods and free goods

REVISED

Economic goods are created from resources that are limited in supply and so are scarce. Consequently, they command a price.

Free goods are unlimited in supply such as sunlight or sand on a beach. Consumption by one person does not limit consumption by others. Therefore, the opportunity cost of consuming a free good is zero.

Now test yourself

TESTED

2 Identify the factor of production in each of the following cases:
   (a) Copper deposits in Zambia.
   (b) A woman who opens a hairdressing salon.
   (c) Machinery used in car production.
   (d) An engineer making computer games for a company.
3 Classify the following into capital and consumer goods:
   (a) A laptop used by a company director for his business.
   (b) A curry eaten by Marie for her lunch.
   (c) A visit to a spa by Kirsten.
   (d) A car used to transport a manager between offices.
4 Why do societies have to make choices about what to produce?
5 If a person's top two priorities are a holiday in Greece and a new a home cinema system but he only has enough money for one of these, what would be the opportunity cost of purchasing the home cinema system?
6 Why does the consumption of free goods not incur an opportunity cost?

Answers on p. 108

Production possibility frontiers (PPFs)

A **production possibility frontier** (PPF) shows combinations of two goods which could be produced by an economy if all its resources were employed fully and efficiently. Figure 1.1 shows a PPF.

In constructing the following PPF it is assumed that the economy can produce either consumer goods or capital goods. **Capital goods** are those required to produce other goods — both capital and consumer goods. Examples include machinery, factory buildings. **Consumer goods** are those that give satisfaction (or utility) to consumers, e.g. smartphones, curry and cars.

A **production possibility frontier** illustrates the maximum potential output of an economy when all resources are fully employed.

Exam tip

To avoid confusion between capital goods and consumer goods, consider how they are used: anything which is an aid to production is classified as a capital good, whereas anything used by someone for final consumption is classified as a consumer good.

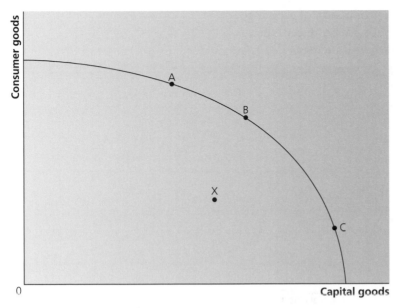

Figure 1.1 A production possibility frontier (PPF)

By definition, any point on the PPF, e.g. A, B or C, implies that all resources are fully and efficiently employed. Therefore, all points on the PPF indicate **the maximum productive potential of an economy and that resources are being used efficiently**.

However, if the economy was operating inside its PPF, e.g. at point X, then it would indicate that there are unemployed resources in the economy. For example, some workers may be unemployed or machinery may be unused. It could also imply that **resources are not being allocated efficiently**.

Possible and unobtainable production

Any points inside, or on the PPF, represent combinations of the two products which are obtainable.

However, any points to the right of the PPF would be currently unobtainable. They could only become obtainable if there was economic growth.

PPFs and opportunity cost

- The PPF is drawn as a curve (concave to the origin) in Figure 1.1.
- This may be analysed in terms of the concept of opportunity cost and marginal analysis.
- **Marginal analysis** involves consideration of the impact small changes make on the current situation.
- Therefore, a marginal increase in the output of capital goods means that some consumer goods must be sacrificed (the opportunity cost).
- In Figure 1.2, when output of capital goods is increased from 0M to 0S, the output of consumer goods is reduced from 0L to 0R.
- Therefore, the opportunity cost of increasing the output of capital goods by MS is LR consumer goods.
- Since the PPF has been drawn as a curve, it can be seen that as output of capital goods is further increased, e.g. by SV, the opportunity cost rises, i.e. by RT consumer goods. The main reason for this is that some resources will be better suited to the production of consumer

> **Marginal analysis** is concerned with the impact of additions to or subtractions from the current situation. The rational decision-maker will only decide on an option if the marginal benefit exceeds the marginal cost.

> **Exam tip**
>
> If the PPF was a straight line then the opportunity cost would be constant.

goods, while others are better suited to the production of capital goods. Therefore, when more and more capital goods are produced, the opportunity cost in terms of consumer goods will increase.

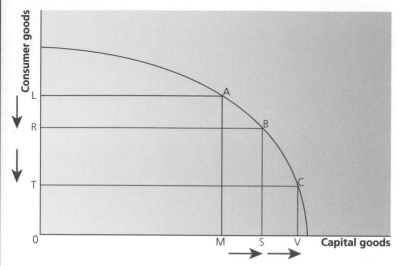

Figure 1.2 Production possibility frontiers and opportunity cost

Production possibility frontiers (PPFs), economic growth and economic decline

REVISED

PPFs may be used to illustrate **economic growth**.

- Look at Figure 1.2. Suppose that the economy is currently operating at point A on the PPF with 0L consumer goods and 0M capital goods being produced.
- It is also assumed that the 0M capital goods produced are just sufficient to replace worn-out machinery.
- If there is a reallocation of resources so that the production of capital goods is increased to 0S, then only 0R consumer goods can now be produced.
- Therefore, the opportunity cost of producing MS more capital goods is LR consumer goods.

This reduction in the output of consumer goods implies a fall in current living standards. However, in the long run, there will be economic growth because the extra capital goods will cause an increase in the productive capacity of the economy resulting in a rightward shift in the PPF as shown in Figure 1.3.

> **Economic growth** refers to an increase in the productive capacity of the economy indicating an increase in real output.
>
> **Economic decline** refers to a decrease in the productive capacity of the economy indicating a decrease in real output.

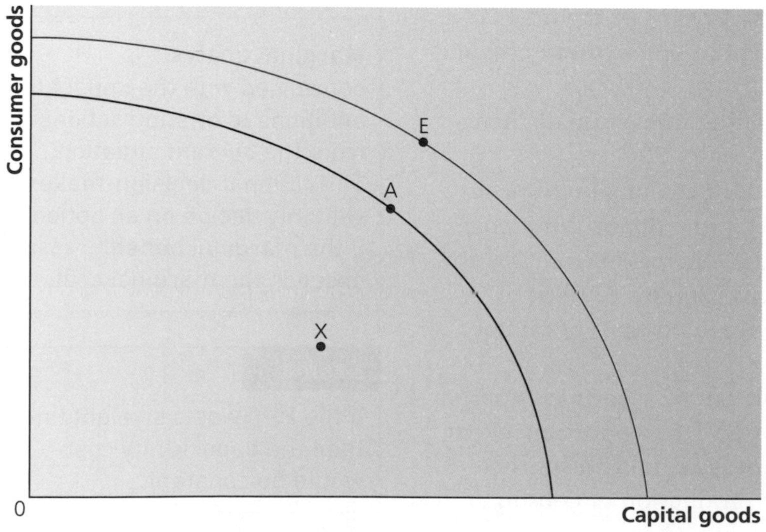

Figure 1.3 Production possibility frontiers and economic growth

It can be seen that if the economy moved from point A to point E then more of both capital goods and consumer goods could be produced. In turn, this implies that living standards would increase in the long run.

In contrast, **economic decline** would be associated with an inward shift in the PPF and might have occurred as a result of resources being reallocated from the production of capital goods to the production of consumer goods, e.g. if the production of capital goods was reduced below 0M then there would be insufficient production of capital goods to cover depreciation so reducing the productive capacity of the economy. This would cause an inward shift in the PPF. Other factors causing shifts in the PPF are outlined below.

Movements along a PPF and shifts in PPFs

REVISED

Changes in the combination of the two goods being produced e.g. capital goods and consumer goods would cause movements *along* a given PPF. Such a change might occur if the economy devoted more resources to the production of capital goods and fewer to the production of consumer goods. This would involve an opportunity cost (see section above on PPF and opportunity cost).

There are a range of factors which could cause a shift in the whole PPF. These are outlined in the following two sections.

Factors causing an outward shift in the PPF

REVISED

Factors which might cause an outward shift in the PPF include:
- discovery of new natural resources, e.g. oil
- development of new methods of production which increase productivity
- advances in technology
- improvements in education and training which increase the productivity of the workforce
- factors which lead to an increase in the size of the workforce, e.g. immigration, an increase in the retirement age, better childcare enabling more women to join the workforce

Factors causing an inward shift in the PPF

REVISED

Factors which might cause an inward shift in the PPF include:
- natural disasters, e.g. earthquakes, floods which cause a destruction of productive capacity
- depletion of natural resources
- factors causing a reduction in the size of the workforce, e.g. emigration, an increase in number of years spent in compulsory education
- a deep recession that results in a loss of productive capacity with factories closing down permanently

> **Exam tip**
>
> Remember that the PPF represents the possible outputs of two goods which could potentially be produced. Points on the PPF do not represent what is actually produced unless all resources are fully employed.

Now test yourself

TESTED

7 With reference to the diagram below:

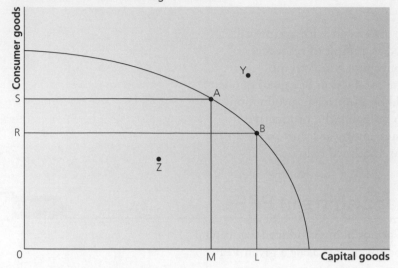

(a) What does point Z represent?

(b) Under what circumstances could the combination of goods at point Y be achieved?

(c) What is the opportunity cost of increasing the output of consumer goods by RS?

(d) How might this affect:

    (i) present living standards, and

    (ii) future living standards?

8 What will be the effect on a PPF of each of the following:

(a) improvements in education and training leading to an increase in labour productivity

(b) a tsunami in Japan which caused the closure of nuclear power stations

(c) an increase in the amount of capital per worker

(d) an increase in immigration of people aged between 16 and 65

Answers on p. 108

Specialisation and the division of labour

The meaning of the division of labour

REVISED

This occurs when workers specialise in very specific tasks, i.e. the work is divided up into many smaller parts so that each worker is responsible for a very small part of the product or service being provided.

> **Division of labour** occurs when the work is split up into small tasks.

Adam Smith and the division of labour

REVISED

In *The Wealth of Nations* Adam Smith set out the view that economic growth could be achieved by increasing the division of labour. This involved the breaking down of a task into many small jobs with workers specialising in a particular task without the need to change jobs during the day. This saved time and enabled each worker to become an expert in that task so increasing his or her productivity.

Advantages and disadvantages of specialisation and the division of labour in organising production

Advantages

The following factors help to explain why the division of labour has been widely adopted:

- Each worker specialises in tasks for which he or she is best suited.
- Therefore, he or she only has to be trained in one task.
- Less time is wasted because a worker no longer has to move from one task to another.
- In manufacturing such an approach enables production line methods to be employed and allows an increased use of machinery.
- In turn, this helps to increase productivity and to reduce average costs of production.

> **Typical mistake**
>
> Thinking that division of labour entails increased training costs. In practice, training costs should be reduced because the worker only has to be trained in one particular task.

Disadvantages

Despite the above advantages, certain problems are associated with the division of labour including:

- Monotony and boredom for workers: this could result in a decrease in productivity.
- Loss of skills: workers trained in one particular task have only limited skills. This could be a problem if they are made redundant.
- A strike by one group of workers could bring the entire production facility to a standstill.
- There is a lack of variety because all goods produced on a production line are identical.

Advantages and disadvantages of specialisation to trade

Advantages

If a country specialises in the production of certain goods and services and then trades these in exchange for goods and services that it does not produce, then it can benefit from increased output, greater choice and lower prices.

Disadvantages

Such specialisation might mean that a country becomes over-dependent on imported goods and services. If its goods and services are uncompetitive then unemployment could result, and the country's value of imports may persistently exceed the value of its exports.

Limits to the division of labour

Certain factors will limit the extent to which the division of labour can be applied:

- The size of the market: if there is only a small market then it will be more difficult to specialise.

- The type of the product: for example, designer fashion products are likely to be unique and not suitable for the division of labour.
- Transport costs: if these are high then large-scale production and the division of labour may not be possible.

The functions of money

REVISED

Money performs various functions which help to facilitate specialisation and the division of labour. The key functions are:
- **As a medium of exchange** enabling people to specialise, exchanging the money earned from doing a specialist job for the goods and services they wish to buy.
- **A store of value** enabling people to save in order to buy goods in the future.
- **A measure of value** enabling people to assess the value of different goods and services.
- **A means of deferred payments** enabling people to buy goods and pay for them on credit.

> **Money** refers to anything that is used as a means of exchange for goods and services.

Now test yourself

TESTED

9 Which of the following would make it more difficult for a firm to adopt a greater degree of specialisation?
 (a) increasing sales
 (b) new machinery available
 (c) falling costs of transporting goods to consumers
 (d) production of unique products which are designed to meet individual consumer wishes
10 Explain the importance of money as a medium of exchange.

Answers on p. 108

Free market economies, mixed economy and command economy

Economies may approach the economic problem of scarcity and of answering the questions of what to produce, how to produce, and how the goods produced should be allocated in different ways as described below.

Free market economies

REVISED

The **free market economy** is one in which the above questions are determined by market forces. The main characteristics of such economies are:
- Private ownership of resources.
- Market forces, i.e. supply and demand determine prices.
- Producers aim to maximise profits.
- Consumers aim to maximise satisfaction.
- Resources are allocated by the price mechanism.

In his book *The Wealth of Nations*, written in 1776, **Adam Smith** suggested that when individuals follow their own self-interest, they indirectly promote the good of society. Consequently, the free market economy would result in an ordered market with producers responding to changes in consumer wants in such a way that there was little waste.

Smith believed that the role of the government should be limited to providing public goods such as defence and justice.

In the twentieth century **Frederich Hayek** offered a strong defence of the free market along with support for private property. Further, he argued in his book *The Road to Serfdom* that attempts by governments to determine the answers to the questions what to produce, how to produce and for whom, were doomed to failure. State planning would require force and involve restrictions on freedom.

Now test yourself

11 Identify four characteristics of a free market economy.

Answer on p. 108

Command economy

REVISED

The **command or centrally planned economy** is one in which the above questions are determined by the state. The main characteristics of such economies are:

- Public (state) ownership of resources.
- Price determination by the state.
- Producers aim to meet production targets set by the state.
- Resources are allocated by the state.
- There is greater equality of income and wealth than in a free market economy.

Writing in the nineteenth century, **Karl Marx** thought that capitalism was inherently unstable because workers are exploited by the bourgeoisie (the owners of the factors of production). Ultimately, there would be a proletariat revolution in which communism would result.

Mixed economy

REVISED

The mixed economy is a mixture of the free market economy and the command economy. In practice, there are no absolutely free market or command economies: most are mixed economies. In these economies, some resources are allocated by the price mechanism while others are allocated by the state. What differs between countries is the degree of that mix.

> **Typical mistake**
>
> Assuming that there is government intervention in a free market economy.

> **Exam tip**
>
> A **free market economy** refers to all the buyers and sellers of a product or service who determine its price.
>
> A **command economy or centrally planned economy** is one in which resources are allocated by the state.
>
> A **mixed market economy** is a combination of a free market economy and a command economy.

Advantages and disadvantages of free market economies

Advantages

The main advantages of free market economies include:

- **Consumer sovereignty** — this implies that spending decisions by consumers determine what is produced.
- **Flexibility** — the free market system can respond quickly to changes in consumer wants.
- **No officials** are needed to allocate resources.
- **Competition** and the profit motive help to promote an efficient allocation of resources.
- **Increased choice** for consumers compared with a command economy.
- **Economic and political freedom** for consumers and producers to own resources.

Now test yourself

TESTED

12 What is meant by 'consumer sovereignty'?
13 Outline three other advantages of a free market economy.

Answers on p. 108

Disadvantages

Disadvantages associated with free market economies include:

- **Inequality** — those who own resources are likely to become richer than those who do not own resources.
- **Trade cycles** — free market economies may suffer from instability in the form of booms and slumps.
- **Imperfect information** — consumers may be unable to make rational choices if they have inadequate information or if there is asymmetric information (see p.55).
- **Monopolies** — there is a danger that a firm may become the sole supplier of a product and then exploit consumers by charging prices higher than the free market equilibrium.
- **Externalities** — these are costs and benefits to third parties which are not taken into account when goods are produced and consumed.

> **Exam tip**
>
> When thinking about the advantages and disadvantages of a free market economy, consider the impact on individuals, businesses and the whole economy.

Now test yourself

TESTED

14 Why does inequality occur in a free market economy?
15 Outline three other disadvantages of a free market economy.

Answers on p. 108

Exam practice answers and quick quizzes at **www.hoddereducation.co.uk/myrevisionnotes**

Advantages and disadvantages of command economies

Advantages

The main advantages of command economies include:

- **Greater equality** — the state can ensure that everyone can enjoy a minimum standard of living and that no one is extremely rich.
- **Macroeconomic stability** — the state can ensure that booms and slumps are smoothed out.
- **External benefits and external costs** may be taken into account when planning production.
- **No exploitation** — there is no exploitation of workers and consumers by privately owned monopolies.
- **Full employment** — the state can ensure that all workers are employed.

Disadvantages

Disadvantages associated with command economies include:

- **Inefficiency** — the absence of the profit motive and competition may result in an inefficient allocation of resources.
- **Lack of incentives to take risks** — again the absence of the profit motive may reduce incentives for investment.
- **Restrictions on freedom of choice** — people would be directed into the jobs deemed to be needed by the state.
- **Shortages and surpluses** — if the state miscalculates supply and demand then there may be excess demand and/or excess supply of goods and services.

Now test yourself

16 Who is responsible for allocating resources in a command economy?
17 Identify two advantages of a command economy.
18 Why might there be inefficiency in a command economy?

Answers on pp. 108–9

The role of the state in a mixed economy

The state performs a variety of roles, many of which depend on the political priorities of the ruling party. However, in most economies, the state has a number of key roles which include the following to a greater or lesser degree:

- defence and internal security
- provision of public goods
- provision of essential public services, e.g. education and health
- redistribution of income from the rich to the poor

Revision activity

1 Investigate the characteristics of the North Korean economy and identify which economic system it most closely resembles.
2 Make a list of the characteristics of a mixed economy.
3 Draw up a list of the advantages and disadvantages of a mixed economy.

Exam practice

1 (a) **Statement 1:** 'Child benefit can no longer be received if one person in the household earns more than £60 000 a year.'
   Statement 2: 'Only those people on low incomes should receive child benefit.'
   Which of the following best describes the two statements above?
   A   both statements are positive.
   B   statement 1 is positive and Statement 2 is normative.
   C   both statements are normative.
   D   statement 1 is normative and Statement 2 is positive.   [1]
   (b) With reference to Statement 2 above, explain why economists might disagree about an economic policy.   [3]

2 (a) An increase in specialisation and the division of labour is most likely to:
   A   reduce the amount of machinery used in production
   B   increase the cost of training an individual worker
   C   reduce total output
   D   increase output per worker   [1]
   (b) Explain the disadvantages to an individual worker of having a highly specialist job. [3]

3 (a) Explain two possible problems faced by a command economy.   [3]
   (b) One function of the price mechanism in a free market economy is to:
   A   stabilise prices
   B   enable the government to set prices
   C   ration scarce goods
   D   reduce consumers' surplus   [1]

4 (a) A reason why a person might switch her energy supplier from Company X to Company Y which is supplying gas and electricity more cheaply is that:
   A   She believes that prices charged by Company Y will rise in the future.
   B   She is unable to calculate the potential benefits of switching suppliers.
   C   Company X, her current energy supplier, will reduce its prices next year.
   D   She is behaving rationally.   [1]
   (b) Explain why another person may not switch his energy supplier even though competitors are charging lower prices.   [3]

Answers and quick quizzes online

ONLINE

Summary

You should have an understanding of:
- What economics is.
- The four key factors of production: land, labour, capital and enterprise.
- The meaning of scarcity and the need to make choices.
- The difference between consumer goods and services and capital goods and services.
- The difference between labour intensive production and capital intensive production.
- Opportunity cost and its significance for individuals, firms and the government.
- The distinction between free goods and economic goods.

- Positive and normative economic statements.
- Production possibility frontiers including the ability to draw them accurately.
- The use of PPFs to illustrate opportunity cost and economic growth.
- Factors which can cause an inward or outward shift in the PPF.
- The meaning of specialisation and the division of labour.
- Advantages and disadvantages of the division of labour.
- Free market, command and mixed economies.

2 How markets work

Rational decision making

The standard neoclassical analysis makes two very significant assumptions about the ways in which consumers and firms behave:

- Consumers act rationally by aiming to maximise their **utility** (satisfaction).
- Firms also act rationally by aiming to maximise profits.

These assumptions provide a powerful tool for analysis and much of this chapter explores how this can be applied in theory and in real world examples. The analysis that follows is based on these assumptions and can provide some invaluable insights for businesses and governments. However, some economists have criticised the validity of these assumptions, and this has led to the development of a new branch of economics called 'behavioural economics'. This will be considered at the end of this chapter.

> **Utility** refers to the level of satisfaction a consumer receives from the consumption of a product or service.

Demand

Demand refers to the amount demanded by consumers at given prices over a certain period of time. It is important to include a reference to prices and to the time period in a definition of demand.

Demand is not the same as 'want' — 'wanting' a product which cannot be afforded is not demand. Demand must include the ability to pay for the product or service.

> **Demand** is how much is demanded at each price over a certain period of time.

> **Typical mistake**
>
> Confusing 'want' with 'demand': 'wants' refer to desires, and desires may be unaffordable, whereas 'demand' is backed by money.

Shape of the demand curve

REVISED

Figure 2.1 shows that the demand curve is downward sloping from left to right indicating that more will be demanded as price falls.

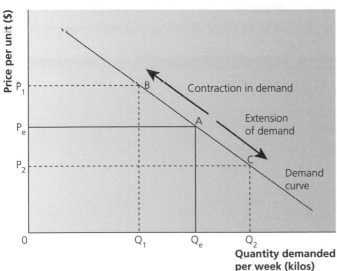

Figure 2.1 Movements along a demand curve

The demand curve demonstrates how a fall in price will cause an increase in the quantity demanded (or an extension in demand) and a rise in price will cause a decrease in quantity demanded (or contraction in demand).

This is based on:
- **The substitution effect:** when there is a rise in price, the consumer (whose income has remained the same) will tend to buy more of a relatively lower-priced good and less of a higher-priced one.
- **The income effect:** when there is a rise in price, consumers will suffer a fall in their real incomes, i.e. purchasing power of their money incomes. With normal goods, the fall in real incomes will reduce the quantity demanded so the income effect reduces the substitution effect.

Movements along the demand curve

REVISED

It may be seen from Figure 2.1 that movements along a demand curve would be caused by price changes. Given that the demand curve has a negative slope, then a rise in price would cause a fall in quantity demanded and a fall in price would cause a rise in quantity demanded.

Revision activity

Construct a demand curve on graph paper based on the following information:

Price per kilo ($)	Quantity of soya demanded per week (kilos)
10	100 000
9	120 000
8	140 000
7	160 000
6	180 000
5	200 000

Shifts in the demand curve

REVISED

Various factors can cause a shift in the whole demand curve. These include changes in:
- **Real incomes.** An increase in real incomes implies that incomes (after discounting the effects of inflation) have increased. This would result in an increase in demand for most goods and services, causing a rightward shift in the demand curve.
- **Size or age distribution of the population.** An increase in the size of the population will cause an increase in demand for most goods and services. An ageing population would cause demand for some goods and services to rise, e.g. sheltered accommodation, and the demand for others to fall, e.g. clothes for teenagers.
- **Tastes, fashions or preferences.** For example, a decrease in the popularity of cabbage will cause a leftward shift in its demand curve.

- **Prices of substitutes or complements.** If there is a change in the price of a related good, it will affect the demand curve for the product. For example, if the price of beef rises, then the demand for a substitute such as lamb will increase. In contrast, if there is a rise in the price of petrol (a complement to cars), then the demand curve for cars would shift to the left.
- **The amount of advertising or promotion.** A successful advertising campaign would cause an increase in demand.
- **Interest rates** affect the cost of borrowing money. For example, a rise in interest rates increases the cost of borrowing money for mortgages, so causing a decrease in demand for houses.

Exam tip

It is only when there is a change in the conditions of demand that the whole demand curve shifts. Price changes cause a movement along an existing demand curve.

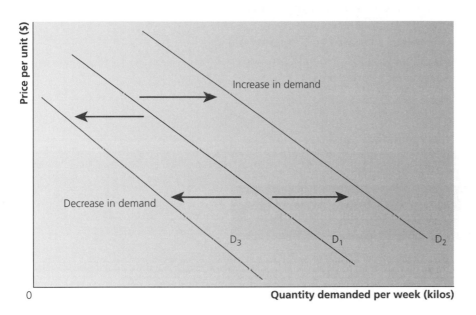

Figure 2.2 Shifts in the demand curve

Figure 2.2 illustrates how an increase in demand would cause the whole demand curve to shift to the right, whereas a decrease in demand would cause the whole demand curve to shift to the left.

The concept of diminishing marginal utility and its influence on the demand curve

REVISED

This principle is based on the idea that consumers gain satisfaction or utility from the goods they consume. **Total utility** represents the total satisfaction gained from the total amount of a product consumed, whereas **marginal utility** represents the change in utility from consuming an additional unit of the product.

The principle of diminishing marginal utility states that, as a person consumes more and more of a product, the marginal utility (extra satisfaction or benefit) falls. Consequently, people are prepared to pay less as their consumption increases with the result that there will be an inverse relationship between the price and quantity demanded.

Total utility is the amount of satisfaction a person derives from the total amount of a product consumed.

Marginal utility is the change in total utility from consuming an extra unit of a product.

The law of diminishing marginal utility states that, as consumption of a product is increased, the consumer's utility increases but at a decreasing or diminishing rate.

The following example shows the utility gained from consuming apples.

Number of apples	Total utility	Marginal utility
1	20	20
2	34	14
3	44	10
4	50	6
5	52	2

The table shows that as a person consumes more and more apples to satisfy her hunger, total utility increases but the marginal utility gained from consuming each extra apple decreases. If monetary values were assigned to marginal utility then it is clear that a rational consumer would be prepared to pay less for each additional apple. This principle provides the basis for the quantity demanded increasing as price falls.

Revision activity

Suppose an increase in the size of the population causes an increase in the demand for soya. Construct a new demand curve on your previous graph based on the following information:

Price per kilo ($)	Quantity of soya demanded per week (kilos)	New quantity of soya demanded per week (kilos)
10	100 000	120 000
9	120 000	140 000
8	140 000	160 000
7	160 000	180 000
6	180 000	200 000
5	200 000	220 000

Now test yourself

TESTED

1 (a) Define the term 'demand'.
   (b) What would be the effect of the following on the demand for houses in the UK?
      (i) an increase in immigration into the UK
      (ii) a decrease in real incomes
      (iii) an increase in the price of rented accommodation
      (iv) a rise in mortgage interest rates

Answers on p. 109

Price elasticity of demand (PED)

Price elasticity of demand is a measure of the responsiveness of quantity demanded for a product to a change in its price.

> **Price elasticity of demand** measures the sensitivity of the quantity demanded of a product to a change in its own price.

Measurement price elasticity of demand

$$PED = \frac{\text{percentage change in quantity demanded}}{\text{percentage change in price}}$$

> **Typical mistake**
>
> Calculating PED using absolute changes rather than percentage changes.

> **Exam tip**
>
> To calculate a percentage change in, say, quantity demanded, it is necessary to divide the change in quantity demanded by the original quantity demanded and multiply the result by 100.

Calculations of PED and interpretation of results

PED will always have a negative value because price and quantity move in opposite directions (since the demand curve is downward sloping).

Examples

Price inelastic demand

Suppose a 100% increase in the price of oil led to a 20% fall in quantity demanded, then PED would be:

$$\frac{-20}{+100} = -0.2$$

Demand is said to be price inelastic (or relatively price inelastic) because a change in price has led to a smaller percentage change in quantity demanded.

When demand is price inelastic, the value of PED will be between 0 and −1.

Price elastic demand

Suppose a 5% decrease in the price of a package holiday to Florida led to a 20% increase in quantity demanded, then PED would be:

$$\frac{+20}{-5} = -4.0$$

Demand is said to be price elastic (or relatively price elastic) because a change in price has led to a larger percentage change in quantity demanded.

When demand is price elastic, the value of PED will be greater than −1.

> **Exam tip**
>
> When considering whether demand is price elastic or price inelastic, compare the percentage changes in price and quantity. If the percentage change in quantity demanded is larger than the percentage price change, then demand is price elastic.

Figures 2.3a and 2.3b illustrate an inelastic and an elastic segment of a demand curve:

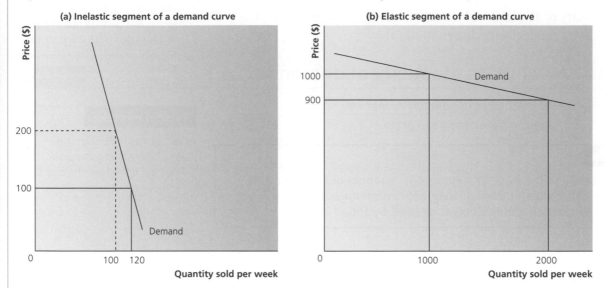

Figure 2.3 An inelastic and an elastic segment of a demand curve

Unit elastic demand

Suppose a 15% decrease in the price of a digital camera led to a 15% increase in quantity demanded, then PED would be:

$$\frac{+15}{-15} = -1.0$$

Demand is said to be unit elastic because a change in price has led to the same percentage change in quantity demanded.

When demand is unit elastic, the value of PED will be equal to 1 and the demand curve will be a rectangular hyperbola (see Figure 2.4).

Perfectly inelastic demand

Suppose a 10% increase in the price of salt led to no change in the quantity demanded, then PED would be:

$$\frac{0}{10} = 0.0$$

Demand is said to be perfectly price inelastic because a change in price has had no effect on quantity demanded.

When demand is perfectly price inelastic, the value of PED will be 0 and the demand curve will be vertical (see Figure 2.4).

Perfectly elastic demand

Suppose a small increase in the price of a product causes the quantity demanded to fall to zero, then demand is said to be perfectly elastic.

When demand is perfectly elastic, the value of PED would be infinity and the demand curve will be horizontal (see Figure 2.4).

> **Exam tip**
>
> Think of perfectly inelastic demand as a set amount demanded whatever the price. The demand curve must therefore be vertical.

Exam practice answers and quick quizzes at **www.hoddereducation.co.uk/myrevisionnotes**

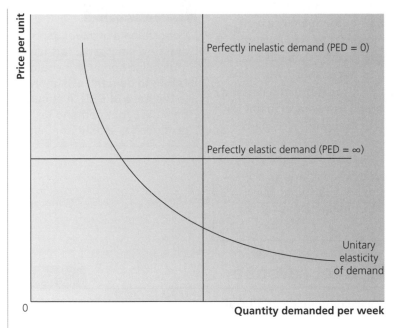

Figure 2.4 Demand curves showing unitary elasticity, perfectly inelastic and perfectly elastic demand

Now test yourself

TESTED

2 Calculate price elasticity of demand in the following examples and comment on your results:
  (a) A rise in the price of electricity from 25 pence to 30 pence per unit causes the quantity demanded to fall from 10000 kilos to 9000 kilos.
  (b) A rise in the price of gold watches from $1000 to $1100 causes demand to fall from 200 to 170 per week.
  (c) A 6% reduction in the price of tomatoes causes a 6% increase in quantity demanded.

Answers on p. 109

Factors influencing price elasticity of demand

REVISED

Factors which influence the price elasticity of demand include:
- **Availability of substitutes:** if substitutes are available there will be a strong incentive to shift consumption to them when the price of the product rises. The existence of substitutes will therefore tend to make demand for the product elastic.
- **Proportion of income spent on a product:** if only a small percentage of income is spent on a product such as salt then demand will tend to be inelastic, whereas if a high percentage of income is spent on the product then demand will tend to be elastic, e.g. exotic holidays and works of art by famous artists.
- **Nature of the product:** if the product is addictive, e.g. alcohol and tobacco, then demand will tend to be inelastic.
- **Durability of the product:** if the product is long-lasting and hard-wearing, e.g. furniture and cars, then demand will be fairly elastic since it is possible to postpone purchases. However, demand for non-durable goods, e.g. milk and petrol, will tend to be inelastic because these must be replaced regularly.

2 How markets work

Edexcel AS/A-level Year 1 Economics A   27

- **Length of time under consideration**: it usually takes time for consumers to adjust their expenditure patterns following a price change. For example, it will take time for motorists to switch from fuel-greedy to more fuel-efficient cars. Consequently, demand is usually more price elastic in the long run than in the short run.
- **Breadth of definition of a product**: if a product is broadly defined, e.g. fruit, demand is likely to be price inelastic. However, demand for particular types of fruit, e.g. apples, is likely to be more price elastic.

> **Typical mistake**
>
> Describing a product as elastic or inelastic: this is imprecise because it could relate to demand or supply. In the case of PED, it should be stated that demand for product X is elastic/inelastic.

> **Exam tip**
>
> It is not helpful to use the idea of luxuries and necessities as a factor influencing price elasticity of demand because what is a necessity or a luxury changes over time. This distinction is far too imprecise to have any value.

Price elasticity of demand and total revenue

REVISED

There are key relationships between price elasticity of demand and **total revenue** (TR):

- When **demand is inelastic**, a price change causes total revenue to change in the **same direction**.
- When **demand is elastic**, a price change causes total revenue to change in the **opposite direction**.
- When **demand is unit elastic**, a price change causes total revenue to **remain unchanged**.
- When **demand is perfectly inelastic**, a price change causes total revenue to change in the **same direction by the same proportion**.
- When **demand is perfectly elastic**, a price rise causes total revenue to **fall to zero**.

> **Total revenue** is the value of goods sold by a firm and is calculated by multiplying price times quantity sold.

> **Typical mistake**
>
> To conclude that if a price change has no effect on total revenue, the demand is perfectly inelastic. This is incorrect: for total revenue to remain constant following a price change, there must have been an exactly proportionate change in quantity demanded. In other words, demand is unit elastic.

> **Revision activity**
>
> The PED varies along a straight-line demand curve. You can check this yourself by completing the following table:

Price per unit (£)	Quantity demanded per week (kilos)	Total revenue	PED
10	10		
9	20		
8	30		
7	40		
6	50		
5	60		
4	70		
3	80		
2	90		
1	100		

Significance of PED for firms

REVISED

If firms know that demand for their product is price inelastic then they know that they can increase total revenue by increasing price.

However, if firms know that demand is price elastic, then they can increase total revenue by reducing price. For example, if there are a lot of restaurants in a high street then one of these might have special offers on certain days, knowing that this will increase its revenue.

Significance of PED for the government

If the government wishes to maximise its tax revenue then it will place indirect taxes on those products whose demand is price inelastic, e.g. goods such as alcohol, petrol and tobacco. However, in this case the consumer will bear most of the tax burden.

The government may therefore also tax products and services whose demand is price elastic, in which case the producers will bear a higher proportion of the tax burden.

Now test yourself

3 If the demand for petrol is price inelastic, what will happen to the total revenue of a garage selling petrol following an increase in price?
4 If a rise in the price of gold jewellery leads to a fall in the total revenue of shops selling this type of jewellery, what can be deduced about price elasticity of demand?
5 An increase in the price of iPads has no effect on total revenue. What can be inferred about the price elasticity of demand?
6 Why is demand for a particular brand of rice likely to be price elastic?
7 Would you expect demand for coffee to be price elastic or inelastic?
8 Why might demand for milk be price inelastic?

Answers on p. 109

Cross elasticity of demand (XED)

The meaning of cross elasticity of demand (XED)

Cross elasticity of demand is a measure of the responsiveness of quantity demanded for one product (Y) to a change in the price of another product (X).

> **Cross elasticity of demand** is the sensitivity of demand for one product to a change in the price of another product.

Measuring cross elasticity of demand

$$XED = \frac{\text{percentage change in quantity demanded of product Y}}{\text{percentage change in price of product X}}$$

Interpreting results

Again for XED, the sign is very significant.
- A **positive sign** indicates that the products are **substitutes**, e.g. a rise in the price of one product will cause an increase in demand for another product.
- A **negative sign** indicates that the products are complements, e.g. a rise in the price of one product will cause a decrease in demand for another product.

> **Typical mistake**
>
> Misinterpreting the result of a calculation of XED. The key point is that if the result is positive, then the goods are substitutes and if negative then the goods are complements.

> **Exam tip**
>
> If the cross elasticity of demand is close to zero then it implies that the products are not closely related.

Value to businesses

A knowledge of cross elasticity of demand is helpful to businesses in setting prices for their products. For example, if the firm is selling a product with a close substitute then it would expect demand for its product to fall considerably if it decided to increase its price.

Firms also know that complementary goods can command high prices. For example, printers are often relatively cheap but the ink cartridges required for them are relatively expensive because a certain type is required for each particular printer.

Income elasticity of demand (YED)

Income elasticity of demand is a measure of the responsiveness of quantity demanded for a product to a change in real income.

> **Income elasticity of demand** is the sensitivity of demand for a product to a change in real income. Note: real income discounts the effects of inflation.

Measuring income elasticity of demand

$$YED = \frac{\text{percentage change in quantity demanded}}{\text{percentage change in real income}}$$

Interpreting results

For YED, the sign is very significant. A **positive sign** indicates that the product is a **normal good**, i.e. a rise (fall) in real income will cause an increase (decrease) in demand.

> **Typical mistake**
>
> Misinterpreting the result of a calculation of YED. The key point is that if the result is positive, then it is a normal good but if the result is negative then the good is an inferior good.

> **Exam tip**
>
> Inferior goods (those with a negative YED) are usually low-quality goods with more expensive substitutes.

> **Examples**
>
> Income elastic demand
>
> If a 5% increase in real income leads to a 25% increase in demand then
>
> $$YED = \frac{25}{5} = +5$$
>
> Demand is income elastic because the change in real income has led to a more than proportionate change in demand. Whenever YED is greater than +1, demand is income elastic.
>
> Income inelastic demand
>
> If a 10% increase in income causes a 3% increase in demand then
>
> $$YED = \frac{3}{10} = +0.3$$
>
> Demand is income inelastic because the change in real income has led to a less than proportionate change in demand. Whenever YED is between 0 and +1, demand is income inelastic.
>
> Inferior goods
>
> A **negative sign** indicates that the product is an **inferior good**, e.g. a rise in real income leads to a fall in demand for the product.
>
> If a 6% increase in real income resulted in a 3% fall in demand then YED would be negative:
>
> $$YED = \frac{-3}{+6} = -0.5$$
>
> As the name suggests, inferior goods are those for which consumption will decline as real incomes increase because consumers can now afford better, higher-quality alternatives.

The relationship between demand and income may be illustrated diagrammatically. For a normal good there is a positive relationship between income and demand but for an inferior good the relationship is negative as shown in Figures 2.5a and 2.5b.

Exam tip

Note that to illustrate normal and inferior goods, income must be on the vertical axis.

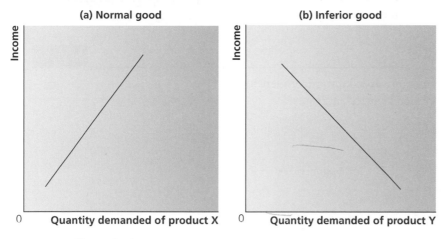

Figure 2.5 The relationship between demand and income

Significance of YED for firms

REVISED

If firms know that demand for their product is income inelastic then they know that demand and total revenue will increase significantly during periods of rapid economic growth but fall significantly during recessions. Consequently, knowledge of income elasticity of demand may be important for firms when making investment decisions.

Significance of YED for the government

REVISED

If the government wishes to maximise its tax revenue during an economic boom it will place indirect taxes on those products whose demand is income elastic. Knowledge of income elasticity of demand might also help the government in estimating tax revenues from indirect taxes on particular goods and services.

Now test yourself

TESTED

9 (a) For each of the following calculate the cross elasticity of demand and comment on your answer:
   (i) A 10% increase in the price of tea causes a 15% rise in the demand for coffee.
   (ii) A 5% increase in the price of product Y causes a 10% decrease in the demand for product X.
 (b) If a 7% increase in the price of good X causes a 7% increase in the demand for good Y then:
   A Goods X and Y are complements.
   B The price elasticity of demand for good X is 1.
   C Goods X and Y and substitutes.
   D Cross elasticity of demand is –1.
10 For each of the following, calculate the income elasticity of demand and comment on your answer:
   (a) A 3% decrease in real incomes causes a 9% fall in the demand for new cars.
   (b) A 5% increase in real incomes causes a 2% fall in demand for soya.
   (c) A 10% increase in real incomes causes a 2% increase in the demand for oranges.

Answers on p. 109

Supply

Supply refers to the amount supplied by producers at given prices over a certain period of time. As with demand, it is important to include a reference to prices and to the time period in the definition.

> **Supply** refers to how much is supplied at each price over a certain period of time.

Shape of the supply curve

Figure 2.6 shows that the supply curve is upward sloping from left to right, indicating that more will be supplied as price increases.

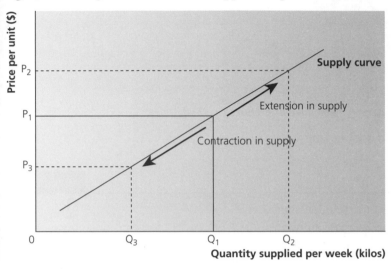

Figure 2.6 Movements along a supply curve

When the price rises it becomes more profitable for producers to supply a product and so they have an incentive to increase production. In contrast, when there is a fall in price it becomes less profitable to supply a product and so firms will reduce output and/or exit the market.

Therefore:
- a rise in price will cause an increase in the quantity supplied (or an extension in supply) and
- a fall in price will cause a decrease in quantity supplied (or contraction in supply).

Revision activity

Construct a supply curve on graph paper based on the following information:

Price per kilo ($)	Quantity of soya supplied per week (kilos)
10	200 000
9	180 000
8	160 000
7	140 000
6	120 000
5	100 000

Exam practice answers and quick quizzes at **www.hoddereducation.co.uk/myrevisionnotes**

Movements along the supply curve

REVISED

It may be seen from Figure 2.6 that movements along a supply curve are caused by price changes. Given that the supply curve has a positive slope, then a rise in price will cause a rise in quantity supplied and a fall in price will cause a fall in quantity supplied.

Shifts in the supply curve

REVISED

Various factors will cause a shift in the whole supply curve. These include changes in:

- **Costs of production.** These include wages, raw materials, energy and rent. An increase in costs of production, such as electricity prices, will cause the whole supply curve to shift to the left.
- **Productivity of the workforce.** Labour productivity refers to the output per worker per hour worked. If there is a rise in productivity then the whole supply curve will shift to the right.
- **Indirect taxes**. An indirect tax raises the cost of supply and so causes the supply curve to shift to the left. A rise in VAT will cause the supply curve to become steeper because it is a percentage of the price of a product, whereas a rise in a specific tax, e.g. 20p per unit, will cause a parallel leftward shift in the supply curve.
- **Subsidies.** These are grants to producers from the government which effectively lead to a reduction in costs of production so causing a rightward shift in the supply curve.
- **Technology.** New invention and new technology usually result in an increase in productivity so causing the supply curve to shift to the right.
- **Discoveries of new reserves of a raw material.** If, for example, a country discovers new oil reserves then the supply curve will shift to the right.

Figure 2.7 illustrates that an increase in supply will cause the whole supply curve to shift to the right, whereas a decrease in supply will cause the whole supply curve to shift to the left.

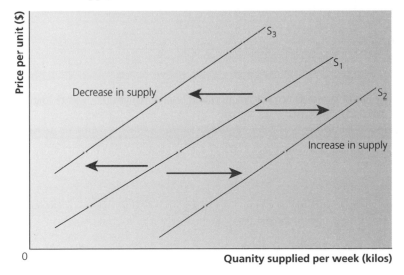

Figure 2.7 Shifts of a supply curve

> **Exam tip**
>
> It is only when there is a change in the conditions of supply that the whole supply curve shifts. Price changes cause a movement along an existing supply curve.

Revision activity

Assume there is a good soya harvest. Construct a new supply curve on graph paper based on the following information:

Price per kilo ($)	Quantity of soya supplied per week (kilos)	New quantity of soya supplied per week (kilos)
10	200 000	220 000
9	180 000	200 000
8	160 000	180 000
7	140 000	160 000
6	120 000	140 000
5	100 000	120 000

Now test yourself

TESTED

11 Define the term 'supply'.
12 What would be the effect of the following on the supply of tea?
    (a) a subsidy to tea producers
    (b) an increase in wages of tea plantation workers
    (c) an increase in productivity of tea workers
    (d) a drought in tea growing regions

Answers on p. 109

Price elasticity of supply (PES)

Price elasticity of supply is a measure of the responsiveness of quantity supplied for a product to a change in its price.

> **Price elasticity of supply** is the sensitivity of supply of a product to a change in its price.

Measuring price elasticity of supply

REVISED

$$PES = \frac{\text{percentage change in quantity supplied}}{\text{percentage change in price}}$$

Interpreting results

PES will always have a positive value because price and quantity move in the same direction (since the supply curve is upward sloping).

Examples

Price inelastic supply

Suppose a 10% increase in the price of wheat led to a 5% increase in quantity supplied, then PES would be:

$$\frac{5}{10} = 0.5$$

Supply is said to be price inelastic (or relatively price inelastic) because a change in price has led to a smaller percentage change in quantity supplied. When supply is price inelastic, the value of PES will be between 0 and 1 (see Figure 2.8).

Price elastic supply

Suppose a 2% decrease in the price of PCs led to 12% decrease in quantity supplied, then PES would be:

$$\frac{12}{2} = 6.0$$

Supply is said to be price elastic (or relatively price elastic) because a change in price has led to a larger percentage change in quantity supplied. When supply is price elastic, the value of PES will be greater than 1 (see Figure 2.8).

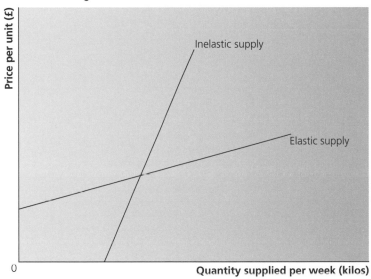

Figure 2.8 Inelastic and elastic supply

Unit elasticity of supply

Suppose a 7% increase in the price of bread led to a 7% increase in quantity supplied, then PES would be:

$$\frac{7}{7} = 1.0$$

Supply is said to be unit elastic because a change in price has led to the same percentage change in quantity supplied. When supply is unit elastic, the value of PES will be equal to 1 and the supply curve will be a straight line drawn through the origin as shown in Figure 2.9.

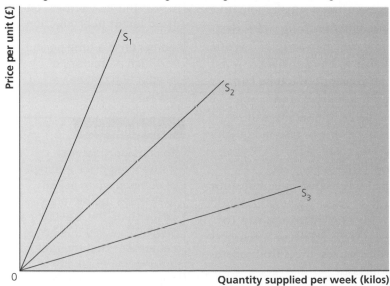

Figure 2.9 Unitary elasticity of supply

Perfectly inelastic and perfectly elastic supply

Suppose a 10% increase in the price of a product led to no change in the quantity supplied, then PES would be

$$\frac{0}{10} = 0.0$$

Supply is said to be perfectly price inelastic because a change in price has had no effect on quantity supplied. When supply is perfectly price inelastic, the value of PES will be 0 and the supply curve will be vertical (see Figure 2.10). On the other hand, if an infinite amount could be supplied at a certain price, then supply is said to be perfectly elastic. When supply is perfectly elastic, the value of PES would be infinity and the supply curve will be horizontal.

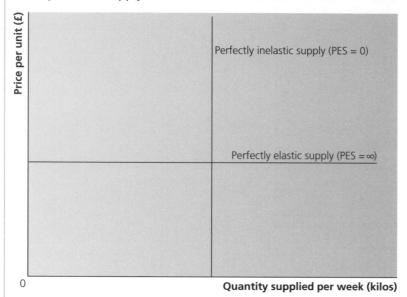

Figure 2.10 Elasticity of supply

Factors influencing price elasticity of supply

REVISED ☐

Factors which influence the price elasticity of supply include:

- **Time.** Elasticity of supply is very likely to vary over time. In economics, the **short run** is defined as that period of time in which at least one factor of production is fixed, whereas the long run is the period of time in which all factors of production are variable. It is often difficult to change supply quickly in response to a price change in the short run, making supply very inelastic. However, in the **long run**, supply is likely to be more elastic because all resources are variable.
- **Stocks.** If stocks of finished goods are available, the supply will be relatively elastic because manufacturers will be able to respond quickly to a price change.
- **Spare capacity**. If a firm has under-utilised machinery and under-employed workers or if it is possible to introduce a new shift or workers, then supply is likely to be elastic.
- **Availability and cost of switching resources from one use to another.** If resources, such as labour, have specific skills or machinery is highly specific, or it is expensive to reallocate resources from one use to another, then supply will be relatively inelastic.

Short run is a time period in which there is at least one fixed factor of production.

Long run is a time period in which all factors of production can be varied.

Typical mistake

To consider factors influencing price elasticity of *demand* when asked to discuss the factors influencing the elasticity of *supply*. To avoid this error, remember that the factors influencing elasticity of supply are those affecting businesses, not consumers.

TESTED

Now test yourself

13 For each of the following calculate the elasticity of supply and comment on your answer:
   (a) A 20% increase in the price of lemons leads to a 2% increase in quantity supplied.
   (b) A 5% fall in the price leads to a 15% reduction in the quantity supplied.
14 Why might you expect the supply of tomatoes to be inelastic?
15 Under what circumstances might the supply of butter be elastic?

Answers on p. 109

Price determination

The **equilibrium** price and output are determined by the interaction of supply and demand (see Figure 2.11).

When the quantity supplied is equal to the quantity demanded of a particular product, equilibrium is said to exist. The equilibrium price and output will not change unless one of the conditions of supply or conditions of demand change.

> **Equilibrium (price and quantity)** is determined by the interaction of the supply and demand curves. The equilibrium price and quantity would not change unless there was a change in the conditions of demand or supply.

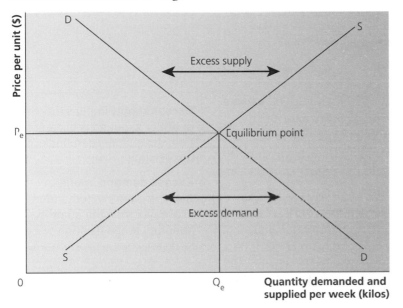

Figure 2.11 Equilibrium price and quantity

> **Typical mistake**
>
> Mislabelling the supply and demand curves. The revision activity should help you to remember that the demand curve is downward sloping from left to right while the supply curve is upward sloping from left to right.

Revision activity

Construct a demand curve and a supply curve on graph paper based on the following information:

Price per kilo ($)	Quantity of soya demanded per week (kilos)	Quantity of soya supplied per week (kilos)
10	100 000	200 000
9	120 000	180 000
8	140 000	160 000
7	160 000	140 000
6	180 000	120 000
5	200 000	100 000

Find the equilibrium point and show the equilibrium price and quantity on your diagram.

> **Exam tip**
>
> Before considering any change in equilibrium price and quantity, you should always begin with a diagram showing the initial equilibrium price and output.

Excess demand and excess supply

Figure 2.12 illustrates what happens if the price is not currently at its equilibrium level.

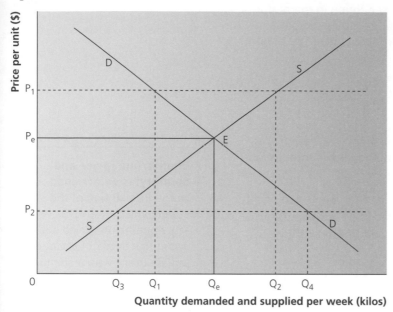

Figure 2.12 Excess demand and excess supply

If the price is above the equilibrium price of P_e then there will be **excess supply**. For example, if the price is at P_1 then the quantity demanded will be only Q_1, while the quantity supplied will be Q_2, so there will be a surplus of Q_1Q_2. Market forces will cause price to fall to P_e which will lead to an extension of demand and a contraction in supply so eliminating the excess supply.

If the price is below the equilibrium price of P_e then there will be **excess demand**. For example, if the price is at P_2 then the quantity demanded will be Q_4 while the quantity supplied will be only Q_3, so there will be a shortage of Q_3Q_4. Market forces will cause price to rise to P_e which will lead to an extension of supply and a contraction in demand so eliminating the excess demand.

> **Excess supply** implies that the quantity supplied is greater than the quantity demanded at the existing price.
>
> **Excess demand** implies that the quantity demanded is greater than the quantity supplied at the existing price.

Now test yourself

16 If the current price is above the free market price, identify whether there is excess supply or excess demand.

17 If the existing market price is above the equilibrium price, explain how equilibrium is restored?

Answers on p. 109

Changes in the equilibrium price

A change in the equilibrium price can be caused by:
- a change in the conditions of demand (which would cause the demand curve to shift) or
- a change in the conditions of supply (which would cause the supply curve to shift)

An increase in demand

This would cause a rightward shift in the demand curve, a rise in price and an increase in the quantity as shown Figure 2.13.

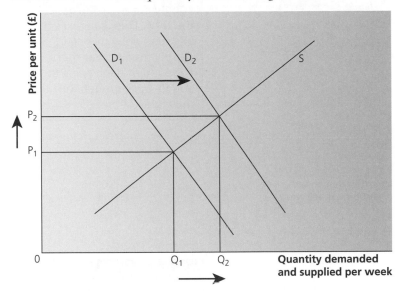

Figure 2.13 An increase in demand

A decrease in demand

This would cause a leftward shift in the demand curve, a fall in price and a decrease in the quantity as shown in Figure 2.14.

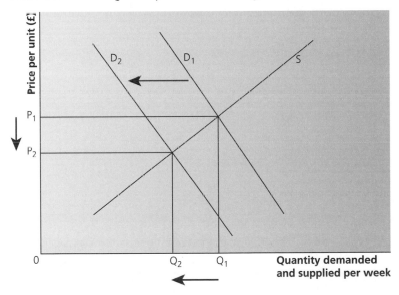

Figure 2.14 A decrease in demand

An increase in supply

This would cause a rightward shift in the supply curve, a fall in price and an increase in the quantity as shown in Figure 2.15.

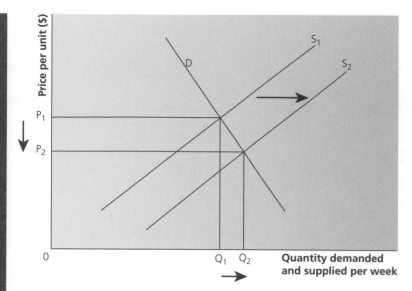

Figure 2.15 An increase in supply

A decrease in supply

This would cause a leftward shift in the supply curve, a rise in price and a decrease in the quantity as shown in Figure 2.16.

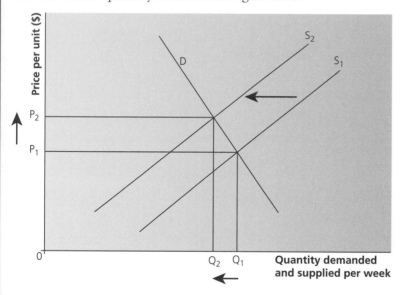

Figure 2.16 A decrease in supply

Now test yourself

TESTED

18 For each of the following explain what happens to the equilibrium price and quantity (you might find it helpful to sketch supply and demand diagrams):
   (a) the effect on the price of beef of a rise in the cost of animal feed
   (b) a change in tastes in favour of blueberries
   (c) an increase in the productivity of workers harvesting rice
   (d) a health scare relating to bananas

Answers on p. 109

The price mechanism

The key functions of the price mechanism in a free market economy may be summarised as follows:

- As a **rationing device** — market forces will ensure that the amount demanded is exactly equal to the amount supplied.
- As an **incentive** — the prospect of making a profit acts as an incentive to firms to produce goods and services.
- As a **signalling device** to producers to increase or decrease the amount supplied.
- To determine **changes in wants** — a change in demand will be reflected in a change in price.

> **Typical mistake**
>
> Assuming that the function of a free market economy is to keep prices stable. While it is true that the forces of supply and demand (market forces) help to determine the equilibrium price, any change in the conditions of supply and demand will cause the equilibrium price to change.

The price mechanism in different types of markets

REVISED

A market refers to all those buyers and sellers of a product or service involved in making exchanges with each other and who help to determine its price. Consequently, markets take on many different forms and do not necessarily operate in one geographical location. They may be local, national or global. For instance, farm shops could be an example of a **local market** since the produce is grown and sold locally. On the other hand, there are **national and/or international markets** for certain goods such as wheat, rice, or certain types of labour, e.g. nurses and teachers. The internet has enabled markets for some goods and services to become much wider because it has made it easier to bring buyers and sellers together.

Consumer and producer surplus

Consumers' surplus

REVISED

This refers to the difference between how much a person is willing to pay and how much they actually pay, i.e. the market price. Diagrammatically, the **consumers' surplus** is the area under the demand curve and above the market price.

Producers' surplus

REVISED

This refers to the difference between how much firms are willing to supply at each price and the market price. Diagrammatically, the **producers' surplus** is the area between the supply curve and the market price.

Figure 2.17 illustrates both consumers' surplus and producers' surplus.

> **Consumers' surplus** is the difference between how much consumers are willing to pay and what they actually pay for a product.
>
> **Producers' surplus** is the difference between the cost of supply and the price received by the producer for the product.

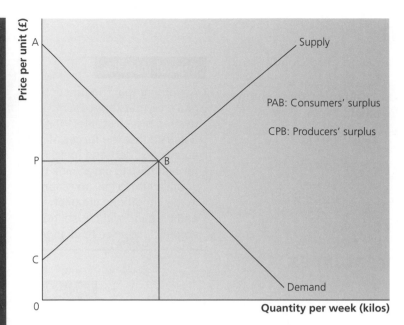

Figure 2.17 Consumers' and producers' surplus

Factors affecting consumers' surplus

REVISED

- The gradient of the demand curve: the steeper it is the greater the consumers' surplus will be.
- Changes in the conditions of demand. For example, an increase in demand will increase the amount of consumers' surplus

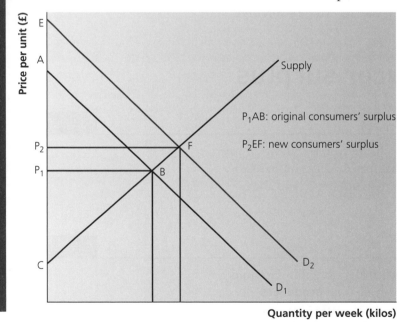

Figure 2.18 Effect of an increase in demand on consumers' surplus

Factors affecting producers' surplus

REVISED

- The gradient of the supply curve: the steeper it is, the greater the producers' surplus will be.
- Changes in the conditions of supply. For example, an increase in supply will increase the amount of producers' surplus. This is illustrated Figure 2.19.

Exam practice answers and quick quizzes at **www.hoddereducation.co.uk/myrevisionnotes**

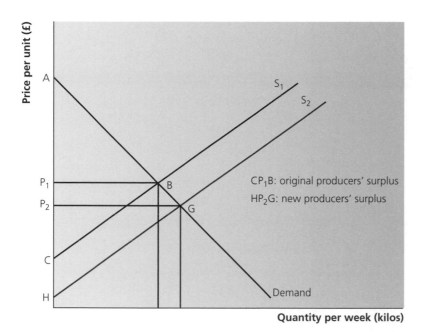

Figure 2.19 Effect of an increase in supply on producers' surplus

Indirect taxes and subsidies

Indirect taxes

REVISED

Indirect taxes are taxes on expenditure and include taxes such as Value Added Tax (VAT), excise taxes and taxes on gambling. Such taxes cause an increase in the cost of supply and so cause the supply curve to shift to the left.

There are two types of **indirect taxes**: *ad valorem* and specific.

> **Indirect taxes** are taxes on expenditure.

Ad valorem taxes

REVISED

Ad valorem **taxes** are a percentage of the price of a product or service and so will cause the supply curve to shift to the left and become steeper than the original supply curve. An example of an *ad valorem* tax is VAT which is currently levied at 20% in the UK.

> *Ad valorem* **taxes** are a percentage of the *price* of the product.

Specific taxes

REVISED

In contrast, a **specific tax** or flat rate tax is a set amount of tax on each unit consumed. Therefore, the effect of a specific tax is to cause the supply curve to shift to the left, parallel to the original supply curve.

Figure 2.20 illustrates the impact of a specific tax when demand is inelastic.

P_1 is the initial equilibrium price and Q_1 is the initial equilibrium output. An indirect tax will cause the supply curve to shift to the left from S_1 to S_2. In turn, this causes the price to increase to P_2 and the quantity to fall to Q_2. It can be seen that when demand is inelastic the consumer bears a much larger proportion of the tax burden (P_1P_2AB), whereas the producer bears a much smaller part of the tax burden (EP_1BC). This distribution of the tax burden is called the **incidence of tax**. The total tax revenue to the government is, therefore, EP_2AC.

> **Specific taxes** are a set amount per unit of the product.
>
> **Incidence of tax** relates to how the burden of a tax is distributed between different groups e.g. producers and consumers.

> **Typical mistake**
>
> Assuming that an indirect tax causes the demand curve to shift to the left.

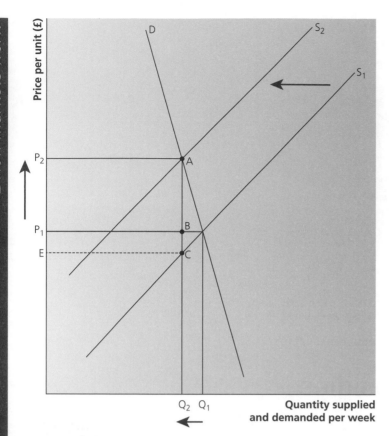

Figure 2.20 Indirect tax when demand is inelastic

In contrast, Figure 2.21 illustrates the impact of a specific tax when demand is elastic.

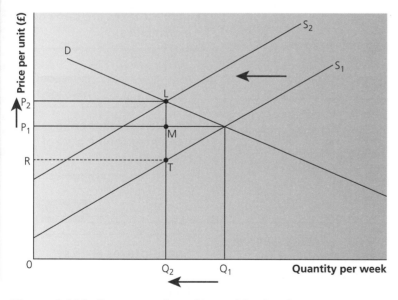

Figure 2.21 Indirect tax when demand is elastic

P_1 is the initial equilibrium price and Q_1 is the initial equilibrium output. An indirect tax will cause the supply curve to shift to the left from S_1 to S_2. In turn, this causes the price to increase to P_2 and the quantity to fall to Q_2. It can be seen that when demand is elastic the producer bears a much larger proportion of the tax burden (RP_1MT), whereas the consumer bears a much smaller part of the tax burden (P_1P_2LM), i.e. the incidence of the tax falls mainly on the producer. The total tax revenue to the government is, therefore, RP_2LT.

Subsidies

A **subsidy** is a grant from the government. These grants have the effect of reducing costs of production. Consequently, subsidies will cause the supply curve to shift to the right. Figure 2.22 illustrates the impact of a subsidy.

> A **subsidy** is a grant from the government which has the effect of reducing costs of production.

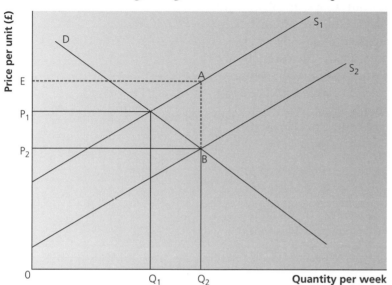

Figure 2.22 The effect of a subsidy

The initial equilibrium price and quantity are P_1 and Q_1 but after the subsidy is granted by the government to producers, the new equilibrium price falls to P_2 and the quantity rises to Q_2. AB represents the subsidy per unit and the total cost of the subsidy to the government is P_2EAB, i.e. the subsidy per unit multiplied by the quantity.

> **Typical mistake**
>
> Shifting the demand curve to right to illustrate the effect of a subsidy. A subsidy affects suppliers and so affects the *supply* curve, not the demand curve.

Now test yourself

19 In 2011, VAT was increased from 17.5% to 20% in the UK. How would this have affected the supply curve for restaurant meals?

Answer on p. 109

Alternative views of consumer behaviour

As indicated at the beginning of this chapter, standard economic analysis makes the assumption that people act rationally and aim to maximise utility. In practice, this assumption may be unrealistic because people's behaviour is subject to a range of influences and motives. **Behavioural economics** applies psychological insights into human behaviour to explain economic decision making.

> **Behavioural economics** is a method of economic analysis that applies psychological insights into human behaviour to explain economic decision making.

Reasons why consumers may not behave rationally

- **Consideration of the influence of other people's behaviour:** much of a person's behaviour is affected and influenced by that of others. Indeed, it is argued that a person subconsciously learns from the behaviour of others as a guide to their own behaviour — a process known as 'social learning'. Examples of how our behaviour is dependent on others might include the clothes and smartphones we buy or the food we eat.

- **The importance of habitual behaviour:** the frequency of our past behaviour influences our current behaviour. Consequently, such behaviour involves little or no thought — it is just done automatically. Habits are difficult to change if they are repeated frequently and if they are associated with rewards which arise quickly after the action. Incentives (which may be financial or non-financial) may be required to change such habits. For example, charging for plastic bags has had a major impact in countries such as Ireland and South Africa.
- **Inertia:** consumers might not make an active effort to change their behaviour for several reasons including:
  ○ information overload
  ○ the complexity of the information available
  ○ too much choice available
  Inertia might arise because people are loss averse, i.e. they will put more effort into preventing a loss than winning a gain. This could explain, for example, why a relatively small proportion of consumers switch their bank accounts or their energy suppliers.
- **Consumer weakness at computation:** people tend to pay more attention to recent events than to distant events when they make decisions. Linked with this, consumers find considerable difficulty in calculating the probability of something happening. They are also influenced by how a choice is presented.

Implications of behavioural economics

REVISED

The points outlined above mean that standard mathematical analysis based on the neoclassical principles of rationality will not accurately describe human behaviour. Consequently, they might have perverse and unintended results when used to formulate policy.

A key implication of this approach therefore is that policy makers need to focus more on the psychology of behaviour when devising policy.

Exam practice

1 (a) A rational consumer will:
   A minimise current consumption
   B maximise satisfaction
   C minimise profits
   D maximise costs of making a decision [1]
   (b) What factors might influence a consumer's decision to buy a product? [3]
2 (a) The law of diminishing marginal utility implies that, as more of a product is consumed by a person:
   A total utility will increase at an increasing rate
   B marginal utility will increase
   C total utility will always be negative
   D marginal utility will decrease [1]
   (b) How does the law of diminishing returns help to explain the shape of the demand curve? [3]
3 (a) The demand curve for iPads will shift to the right if there is:
   A an increase in costs of production
   B a rise in VAT on iPads

C an increase in the productivity of workers producing iPads

D an increase in real incomes of consumers [1]

(b) Identify three reasons why demand for iPads might increase in the future. [3]

4 (a) How might the shape of the supply curve be explained? [3]

(b) The supply curve of potatoes will shift to the left if:

A the cost of fertiliser increases

B there is an increase in advertising of potatoes

C new machinery enables more potatoes to be produced per acre

D the price of rice, a substitute for potatoes, increases in price [1]

5 A baker sells 100 cakes at $5 each on a particular day. When he reduces the price to $4 on the following day, his sales rise to 140 cakes.

(a) Calculate the change in total revenue resulting from the price reduction. [1]

(b) What may be inferred about the price elasticity of demand for cakes? [2]

6 Total expenditure on product X falls as price falls, but demand increases as income falls. Which of the following can be concluded from this information?

	Price elasticity of demand	Income elasticity of demand
A	elastic	negative
B	elastic	positive
C	inelastic	positive
D	inelastic	negative

[1]

7 (a) Product Y has a price elasticity of supply of 0.5. Calculate the change in quantity supplied following a price rise of 30%. [3]

(b) Which of the following could account for this low price elasticity of supply?

A There are no close substitutes for product Y.

B Product Y is addictive.

C Product Y is a heavily advertised brand of coffee.

D The specialist machinery required for product Y is fully utilised. [1]

8 (a) 100 000 jars of jam are demanded per day at £2 a jar. If the price elasticity of demand for these jars is −3 and the price is raised by 10%, the number of jars demanded per day would fall to:

A 60 000

B 70 000

C 80 000

D 90 000 [1]

(b) Explain three factors which might influence the price elasticity of demand for strawberries. [3]

9

Between July 2014 and January 2015 crude oil prices fell from $107 a barrel to $45 a barrel. This was caused by a slowdown in economic growth in rapidly growing economies such as China, very slow growth in the Eurozone and increasing supplies resulting from the shale gas revolution especially in North America.

Lower oil prices have also been accompanied by significant falls in the price of commodities including wheat whose price fell from $330 per tonne in May 2014 to $235 per tonne in February 2015. Oil prices have an impact on wheat prices because oil is required for

transport and is an important source of energy in food production. Wheat prices have also fallen due to:

● countries such as China and Brazil having huge stocks

● larger harvests in Argentina, Russia and the rest of Europe

● fall in demand for wheat for animal feed because corn is now much cheaper following record harvests

Low wheat prices have led to less planting of wheat which might force prices higher by 2016.

(a) Under what circumstances might the short-run supply curve for wheat be price elastic? [4]

(b) Explain the reasons for the fall in the price of crude oil. Illustrate your answer with a supply and demand diagram. [6]

(c) Calculate the percentage change in the price of wheat from the information given in the article. [5]

(d) Assess the impact of a decrease in the price of oil on the market for wheat. [10]

(e) Discuss the factors influencing the income elasticity of demand for oil and wheat. [15]
  EITHER

(f) Evaluate minimum guaranteed price schemes as means of reducing price fluctuations in commodities such as wheat. [20]
  OR

(g) Evaluate the effect of falling wheat prices on consumers and producers. [20]

Answers and quick quizzes online

ONLINE

Summary

You should have an understanding of:
- The assumption of rationality and the reasons why consumers may not behave rationally in practice.
- How a price change causes a movement along a demand curve.
- How changes in the conditions of demand cause shifts in the demand curve.
- How a price change causes a movement along a supply curve.
- How changes in the conditions of supply cause shifts in the demand curve.
- How the equilibrium price and output is determined.
- The causes of changes in the equilibrium price and quantity.
- How market forces will eliminate excess demand and excess supply.
- Price elasticity of demand: how it is calculated and how to interpret the results.
- The factors influencing price elasticity of demand.
- The relationship between price elasticity of demand and total revenue.
- Income elasticity of demand: how it is calculated and how to interpret the results.
- The distinction between normal goods and inferior goods.
- Cross elasticity of demand: how it is calculated and how to interpret the results.
- The distinction between complements and substitutes.
- Price elasticity of supply: how it is calculated and how to interpret the results.
- The factors influencing price elasticity of supply.
- The functions of the price mechanism.
- Consumers' surplus and producers' surplus and the factors influencing each of these concepts.
- The effect of indirect taxes and subsidies using supply and demand analysis.

3 Market failure

Types of market failure

The meaning of market failure

Market failure refers to the failure of the market system to allocate resources efficiently. It arises because the price mechanism has not taken into account all the costs and/or benefits in the production or consumption of the product or service.

> **Market failure** occurs when the forces of supply and demand (market forces) do not result in the efficient allocation of resources.

Types of market failure

There are various reasons why the free market system may fail including:

- externalities: negative externalities and positive externalities
- public goods
- information gaps

These market failures are considered in detail later in this chapter.

> **Exam tip**
>
> Ensure that you know that there are several forms of market failure. The above list is not complete. For example, other forms of market failure include labour immobility, monopoly and inequality but these are not required for the AS specification. These are, however, examined in Themes 3 and 4.

Reasons for market failure

For resources to be allocated efficiently, it is necessary for social marginal costs (SMC) to be equal to social marginal benefits (SMB). In practice, some costs and/or benefits may not be included because they may not be known or difficult to quantify. Social marginal cost refers to the addition to total cost of producing an extra unit of output, whereas social marginal benefit refers to the addition to total benefits of consuming an extra unit.

> **Now test yourself**
>
>
> 1 What is market failure?
> 2 Identity three types of market failure.
> 3 What condition must be met for resources to be allocated efficiently when there are externalities?
>
> **Answers on p. 109**

Externalities

The meaning of externalities

REVISED

These are costs and benefits to third parties who are not directly part of a transaction between producers and consumers. They are, in effect, spillover effects arising from the production or consumption of a product or service which are not taken into account by the price mechanism. **Externalities** are therefore a form of market failure because market forces will not result in an efficient allocation of resources.

> **Externalities** affect parties that are not directly involved in a transaction and may be either costs or benefits.

Types of externality

REVISED

Two types of externality may be distinguished:
- external costs (negative externalities) and
- external benefits (positive externalities)

> **Exam tip**
>
> Think of externalities as effects on stakeholders, e.g. consumers, firms, workers, the government, who are not part of a transaction between others.

Private costs

REVISED

Private costs are those costs paid directly by the producer and consumer in a transaction.
- Private costs of a producer: typically these will include, wages, rent, raw materials, energy.
- Private costs for a consumer: the cost to the consumer is usually the price paid for the product/service.

> **Private costs** are the direct costs to producers and consumers for producing and consuming a product.

External costs (negative externalities)

REVISED

External costs are costs to third parties, i.e. other than to the producer or consumer directly involved in the transaction. They are spillover costs from the production or consumption which the market fails to take into account.

Examples of **external costs of production** include:
- air pollution, e.g. noxious gases from a factory
- noise pollution, e.g. from building work associated with a new factory or from machinery used in the production process
- pollution arising from the destruction of the rain forest to grow crops

Examples of **external costs of consumption** include:
- Passive smoking, i.e. a non-smoker might suffer from adverse health effects if he/she is in the presence of a smoker over a period of time.
- Overeating by individuals: obesity might result in significant costs for the National Health Service and, in turn, taxpayers.

> **External costs** are the costs in excess of private costs that affect third parties who are not part of the transaction.

Social costs

REVISED

Social costs are simply the sum of private costs and external costs. So:

social costs = private costs + external costs

Therefore:

external costs = social costs − private costs

> **Social costs** are the sum of private costs and external costs.

Analysis of external costs of production

REVISED

Figure 3.1 illustrates the welfare loss occurring from the production of a good, which results in external costs to third parties.

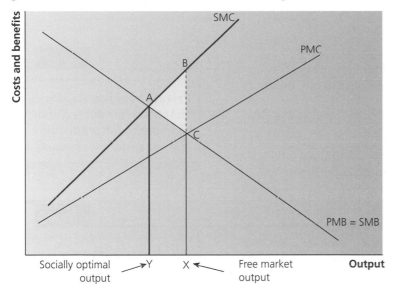

Figure 3.1 External costs of production

- In Figure 3.1, the private marginal benefit curve (PMB) is the demand curve and indicates that private benefits to the consumer decrease as consumption increases. In this case, it is assumed that there are no external benefits so the PMB will be the same as the social marginal benefit (SMB) curve.
- The private marginal cost (PMC) curve is the supply curve and indicates that private costs of providing the product rise as output rises.
- In a free market economy, therefore, the equilibrium will be determined from the equilibrium point at which PMB = PMC, which will be output 0X.
- However, 0X would not be the socially optimal level of output because no account has been taken of the external costs of production.
- The social marginal cost (SMC) curve includes both the private costs and external costs and is, therefore, drawn to the left of the PMC curve.
- The socially optimal level of output is determined from the equilibrium point at which SMC = SMB which will be 0Y.

Welfare loss

- It can be seen that in a free market economy there is over-production and over-consumption of XY.
- This results in a welfare loss, shown as ABC in Figure 3.1.

Now test yourself

4 A firm producing chemicals pays another firm for its raw materials and pays an average wage of £35 000 to its workers. It discharges its waste into a river adjacent to the factory, which causes the fish to die. Fishermen downstream suffer from a loss of income. Farmers pay the chemical company £100 per kilo for the fertiliser produced by the chemical company.
In the above extract, which are private costs and which are external costs?

Answers on p. 109

Private benefits

Private benefits are those benefits that are received directly by the producer and consumer in a transaction.
● Private benefits to a producer: typically these will include the revenues received from the sale of the product/service.
● Private benefits to a consumer: the utility(satisfaction) gained by the consumer from the consumption of the product/service.

> **Private benefits** are direct benefits to producers and consumers for producing and consuming a product.

External benefits

External benefits are benefits to third parties, i.e. other than to the producer or consumer directly involved in the transaction. They are spillover benefits from the production or consumption which the market fails to take into account.

Examples of **external benefits of consumption** include:
● individuals deciding to have vaccinations preventing the spread of disease to others
● households with well-kept gardens increasing the market value of neighbouring properties

Examples of **external benefits of production** include:
● A farmer who keeps bees to make honey. The bees will benefit surrounding farmers by pollinating their crops.
● A firm trains workers in computing skills. Other firms that do not train workers might benefit from employing workers from this firm.

> **External benefits** are benefits in excess of private benefits which affect third parties who are not part of the transaction.

Social benefits

Social benefits are simply the sum of private benefits and external benefits. So:

social benefits = private benefits + external benefits.

Therefore:

external benefits = social benefits − private benefits

> **Social benefits** are the sum of private benefits and external benefits.

Analysis of external benefits of consumption

Figure 3.2 illustrates the welfare loss that occurs due to the consumption of a good, which results in external benefits to third parties.

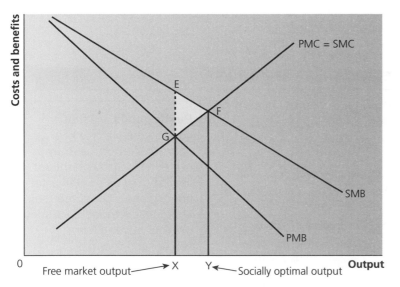

Figure 3.2 External benefits of consumption

- In Figure 3.2, the private marginal benefit curve (PMB) is the demand curve and indicates that private benefits to the consumer decrease as consumption increases.
- The private marginal cost (PMC) curve is the supply curve. In this case, it is assumed that there are no external costs, so the PMC will be the same as the social marginal cost (SMC) curve.
- In a free market economy, therefore, the equilibrium will be determined from the equilibrium point at which PMB = PMC which will be output 0X.
- However, 0X would not be the socially optimal level of output because no account has been taken of the external benefits of production.
- The social marginal benefit (SMB) curve includes both the private benefits and external benefits and is, therefore, drawn to the right of the PMB curve.
- The socially optimal level of output is determined from the equilibrium point at which SMC = SMB which will be 0Y.

Welfare gain

- It can be seen that in a free market economy there is under-production and under-consumption of XY.
- If the socially optimum output is produced, then there will be a welfare gain, shown as EFG in Figure 3.2.

> **Typical mistake**
>
> Welfare gain area identified incorrectly. To avoid this error, remember that at the free market output, the social marginal benefit is greater than the social marginal cost — use this information to determine the welfare loss.

5 It has been estimated that an economics graduate can earn significantly more than a student with two A-levels. Research suggests that graduates secure more interesting and satisfying jobs than non-graduates. A highly skilled workforce might attract more foreign direct investment. Further, graduates learn transferable skills that can help to increase productivity. Both these factors, therefore, help to increase economic growth of the country.
In the above extract, which are private benefits and which are external benefits?

Answers on p. 110

Public goods

The difference between public and private goods

REVISED

The characteristic which makes **public goods** unique is that the benefit that they provide affects many people rather than just one individual. Pure public goods have two special characteristics which distinguish them from private goods:

- **Non-rivalrous:** this means that consumption by one person does not limit consumption by others, i.e. the benefit to others is not reduced by one person's consumption.
- **Non-excludability:** this means that if a good is available for one person, then it is available for everyone, i.e. it is impossible to prevent or exclude anyone from using it.

This is in contrast to **private goods** which are rival and excludable, i.e. consumption by one person means that it cannot be consumed by anyone else and that it is not available to anyone else.

> **Public goods** are those good that have two key characteristics, i.e. they are non-rivalrous (amount available does not fall after one person's consumption) and non-excludable (cannot prevent anyone from consuming them).

Examples of public goods

REVISED

It is arguable whether there are any examples of pure public goods displaying the characteristics of those described above, but examples commonly used include:

- street lighting
- nuclear defence systems
- national parks

The free rider problem

REVISED

These characteristics mean that when a public good is provided by someone, other people will be able to benefit from it without paying — in other words, they get a '**free ride**'. This is a problem because in such circumstances the market will fail: an insufficient number of people will be willing to pay for the product and it will not be profitable for a business to provide it.

> **Free rider problem** is the problem that once a product is provided it is impossible to prevent people from using it and, therefore, impossible to charge for it.

Typical mistake

Assuming that all goods provided by the state, such as health and education, are public goods. This is not necessarily true because health and education are also provided by the private sector.

Now test yourself

TESTED

6 How do private goods differ from public goods?
7 Why does the free rider problem occur?
8 If a person buys a television, it is not possible the prevent him using it whether or not he has a television licence. How do the authorities try to make this an 'excludable' service?

Answers on p. 110

Exam practice answers and quick quizzes at **www.hoddereducation.co.uk/myrevisionnotes**

Information gaps

Symmetric and asymmetric information

The free market system is based on the assumption that consumers and producers make rational choices and decisions based on perfect and equal market knowledge. In practice, this assumption may be unrealistic. For example, producers may have more information than consumers about a product or service, or consumers may simply not have sufficient information to make a rational decision. As a result of this **asymmetric information**, resources may be allocated inefficiently resulting in market failure.

> **Symmetric information** is where both parties in a transaction have the same information.
>
> **Asymmetric information** is where one party in a transaction has more or superior information compared to another.

Examples of asymmetric information

The following provide some examples of markets in which asymmetric information is possible:

- **Housing market:** estate agents may know more about the potential problems of a house than the potential buyer.
- **Life insurance:** the consumer may not reveal all aspects of his health profile to the insurance company, making it difficult for the firm to assess the risk.
- **Second-hand car sales:** the car salesperson will know more about the car than a potential buyer.
- **Financial services:** a bank may be unaware of the likelihood of a default by the borrower.
- **High-tech products:** consumers are unlikely to have as much information as producers about products such as smart phones and pharmaceuticals.

> **Exam tip**
>
> Remember that asymmetric information and incomplete information are a form of market failure because they restrict the ability of consumers and producers to make rational choices.

Now test yourself

9 What information gaps might exist between a dentist and her patient?

Answer on p. 110

Exam practice

1 An oil freighter runs aground not far from a seaside resort. Damage to the freighter causes a major oil spillage which ruins the beaches of the resort. This deters tourists many of whom cancel their bookings at local hotels.

   (a) Using examples from the above extract, distinguish between the private costs and external costs. [3]

   (b) The above example illustrates that:

   A   Social costs are less than external costs.

   B   Private costs are greater than social costs.

   C   External costs are less than private costs.

   D   Social costs are greater than private costs. [1]

2 (a) Public goods are:
   A provided without any opportunity cost
   B only used by producers
   C under-provided by the private sector
   D only provided to those on low incomes [1]
  (b) National defence and street lights are usually provided by the state and financed from tax revenues.
   Explain the characteristics of public goods and how they differ from private goods. [3]

3

It has been estimated that an economics graduate can earn significantly more than a student with two A-levels. Research suggests that graduates secure more interesting and satisfying jobs than non-graduates. A highly skilled workforce might attract more foreign direct investment. Further, graduates learn transferable skills which can help to increase productivity. Both these factors, therefore, help to increase economic growth of the country.

Tuition fees were increased from £3375 in 2011 to £9000 in 2012. This resulted in a 10% fall in applications to English universities. The government argued that private benefits of going to university are significant, so the increase in fees is justified. Free market economists suggest that government subsidies to universities encourage inefficiency and a lack of responsiveness to market demand. Further, many courses may have no benefits to the economy.

(a) What might be the opportunity cost to the government of funding universities? [4]
(b) Explain why university education is not a public good. [5]
(c) Giving examples, explain the private costs for an individual student of a university education. [6]
(d) Assess the private and external benefits of university education. [15]
(e) From the information provided, calculate the price elasticity of demand for university education. Critically examine your result. [10]
   EITHER
(f) Evaluate the economic arguments for an increase in university tuition fees. [20]
   OR
(g) Evaluate the extent to which information gaps make it difficult for a student to decide whether to go to university. [20]

Answers and quick quizzes online

ONLINE

Summary

You should have an understanding of:
- The meaning of market failure.
- Three types of market failure: externalities, public goods and information gaps.
- External costs and external benefits.

- Diagrams depicting external costs of production and external benefits of consumption.
- Public goods: key characteristics non-rivalrous and non-excludability; the free rider problem.
- Information gaps: meaning and significance.

4 Government intervention

Government intervention in markets

Indirect taxes

Indirect taxes are taxes on expenditure and include taxes such as Value Added Tax (VAT), excise taxes and taxes on gambling. Such taxes cause an increase in the cost of supply and so cause the supply curve to shift to the left. As outlined in chapter 2 page 43, there are two types of indirect taxes: *ad valorem* and **specific**.

Governments intervene in a variety of ways, one of the most common of which is through indirect taxes, which are taxes on expenditure. This method may be used to deal with external costs such as pollution. The aim of indirect taxes is to **internalise the externality** by taxing the product so that output and consumption will be at the level at which SMB = SMC. This is illustrated in Figure 4.1.

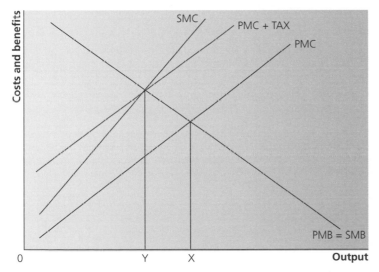

Figure 4.1 The taxing of a firm producing external costs

It can be seen that the tax will cause a leftward shift in the supply curve. If judged correctly, the tax will cause consumption and output to fall to 0Y, the socially optimum level.

Advantages

- incentive to reduce pollution
- source of revenue for the government and few costs administering this method

Disadvantages

- ineffective in reducing pollution if demand is price inelastic
- difficulty of setting an appropriate tax because of the problem of quantifying the external cost

> **Exam tip**
>
> Indirect taxes affect the costs of production and so cause shifts in the *supply* curve and not the demand curve.

Now test yourself

1 How does an internal tax on a producer causing pollution 'internalise the externality'?
2 Why is it difficult to determine how much tax to place on a company whose production causes external costs?
3 Nitrogen from diesel fumes is widely believed to cause undesirable health effects. Draw a supply and demand diagram to illustrate the impact of an increase in VAT on diesel. Show the area of tax borne by:
   (a) the consumer and
   (b) the producer

Answers on p. 110

Subsidies

The government might provide grants to producers to lower production costs so that the product or service can be provided at a lower price. This method may be used to deal with the issue of external benefits. In turn, this should encourage consumption so that it reaches the socially optimal level.

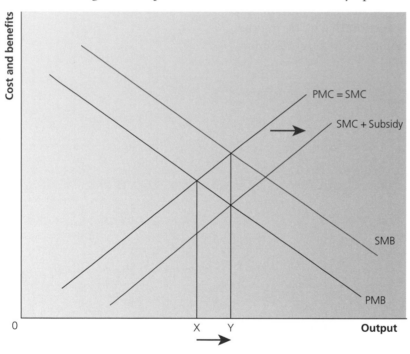

Figure 4.2 A subsidy to encourage consumption of a product which has external benefits

It can be seen that the **subsidy** will cause a rightward shift in the supply curve. If judged correctly, the subsidy will cause consumption and output to rise from 0X to 0Y, the socially optimum level.

> **Subsidies** are government grants to businesses that reduce production costs causing a rightward shift in the supply curve.

Advantages

● reduction in cost of production enabling suppliers to reduce the price
● incentive for people to increase consumption

Disadvantages

● cost to the taxpayer of providing subsidies
● ineffective in increasing consumption if demand is inelastic
● difficulty of setting an appropriate subsidy because of the problem of quantifying the external benefit

Exam practice answers and quick quizzes at **www.hoddereducation.co.uk/myrevisionnotes**

Now test yourself

4 Explain the effect of a decrease in the subsidy for wind farms.

Answer on p. 110

Maximum prices

REVISED

Maximum price controls or price ceilings have been used by governments in a variety of contexts, e.g on rented accommodation, for wages of rugby league players and for items of food.

Figure 4.3 illustrates the effects of a maximum price scheme.

> A **maximum price** is a price, usually set by the government, which makes it illegal for firms to charge more than a certain price for a given quantity of a product.

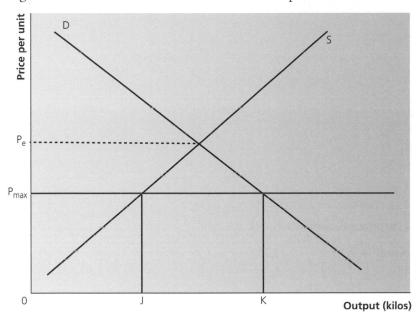

Figure 4.3 A maximum price set below the equilibrium price

- The equilibrium price is P_e.
- Suppose the government sets a maximum price (P_{max}) below the equilibrium price. This will result in a shortage of JK kilos.

The shortage could result in a black market in which those with supplies of the product sell it illegally at a price significantly higher than the maximum price.

Advantages

- They enable consumers on low incomes to be able to afford to buy a product.
- They help to prevent an increase in the country's rate of inflation.

Disadvantages

- There is a danger that shortages mean that some consumers are unable to find supplies of the product.
- Producers may exit the market in order to use their resources to produce goods that are more profitable.
- If the government subsidises producers to encourage them to maintain output, then there will be a significant cost to the taxpayer.

Minimum prices

Minimum prices may be used in a variety of ways. For example, many countries have a national minimum wage. In terms of commodities and food, a government may set a **minimum guaranteed price** (MGP) for a particular commodity. This means that producers know in advance that they will receive a certain price per kilo no matter how much is produced. This is designed to ensure greater certainty and, therefore, act as an incentive to producers to supply sufficient quantities of the commodity.

Figure 4.4 illustrates the effects of a guaranteed minimum price scheme.

> **Minimum guaranteed price** is a price, usually set by the government, which is guaranteed to producers.

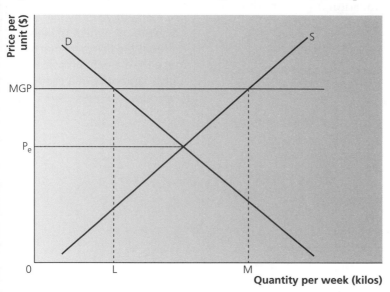

Figure 4.4 A minimum guaranteed price scheme

- The equilibrium price is P_e.
- Suppose the government sets a minimum guaranteed price (MGP) above the equilibrium price. This will result in a surplus of LM kilos.
- The government will buy this surplus and store it for times in which there is a shortage.

Advantages

The advantages of minimum guaranteed price include:
- Producers know in advance the price they will receive for their product.
- This greater certainty enables producers to plan investment and output.

Disadvantages

The problems associated with minimum guaranteed prices are similar to those of buffer stock schemes:
- If the minimum guaranteed price is set too high, then there will be surpluses each year.
- These schemes involve costs of storage which must be borne by taxpayers.
- These schemes encourage over-production and may, therefore, result in an inefficient allocation of resources.

Minimum prices might also be set for some products sold by retailers in order to deter consumption. For example, Scotland plans to impose a minimum retail price for alcohol which is designed to make it less affordable and so reduce consumption.

Exam practice answers and quick quizzes at **www.hoddereducation.co.uk/myrevisionnotes**

Now test yourself

5 What is the main purpose of a guaranteed minimum price for a product such as wheat?
6 Explain the effect on quantity demanded and quantity supplied of a guaranteed minimum price that is set above the free market price.

Answers on p. 110

Tradable pollution permits

Tradable pollutions permits is another method used to reduce external costs. Permits are issued by the government to firms that allow them to pollute up to a certain limit. Any pollution above this limit is subject to fines. The key to this system is that the permits may be traded between firms so that firms that are 'clean' can sell their surplus permits to firms which are more polluting.

> **Tradable pollution permits** (according to the OECD) are rights to sell and buy actual or potential pollution in artificially created markets.

Advantages

- These schemes work through the market mechanism.
- They are an incentive for firms to reduce pollution.
- The costs of administering these schemes are low relative to those associated with systems of regulation.

Disadvantages

- Pollution will continue, albeit at a lower level than previously.
- Large, efficient firms might buy up the permits and continue to pollute.

State provision of public goods

The usual policy response to the lack of provision of public goods by the free market is for the government to provide them financed through taxation. The most obvious benefit is that this ensures that the product or service is provided.

However, a disadvantage of this approach is that ultimately politicians will determine the amount of resources allocated to these public goods without direct reference to the electorate.

Alternative methods of providing some public goods are via agencies appointed by the government (contracting-out) or by charities and voluntary organisations.

Provision of information

Information gaps may be closed by publications in the media, on the internet and written publications which are designed to inform consumers about issues concerning products and services. Examples include information:

- for parents aimed at encouraging them to have their children vaccinated against measles
- about the health risks associated with smoking
- about opportunities for apprenticeships and courses available in higher education

Obviously there is a cost associated with this and there is no guarantee that the policy will be effective.

Regulation

REVISED

Legal regulations can be imposed on the activities of consumers and producers. Such measures include:

- A complete ban on the production of the good or provision of the service.
- Regulations which place limits on the production process or on the amount of pollution allowed.
- Regulations relating to the consumption of a product, e.g. the prohibition of smoking in public places or the age limit on buying cigarettes.

In theory, this should restrict the activity to the required level but without enforcement firms may not meet the legal requirements.

Advantages

- Regulation can limit the extent of the activity.
- It might act as an incentive to producers to develop new technologies that avoid the activity.

Disadvantages

- The cost of enforcement of laws/regulations, e.g. inspectors may have to be employed to ensure that producers and/or consumers abide by the rules.
- Problems of determining the socially efficient levels of the production process or activity.

Property rights

REVISED

Another form of regulation, which can be used to deal with external costs, is the extension of **property rights**. This involves assigning ownership (property) rights to those who might be affected by external costs. This means that owners are given the right to claim damages against those causing the external cost.

> **Property rights** are the exclusive authority to determine how a resource is used, whether that resource is owned by government, collective bodies, or by individuals. In other words, property rights are ownership rights.

Advantages

- Property rights act as an incentive for firms to take into account both the private costs and the external costs.
- The opportunity to fine firms caught polluting and use the money to compensate those damaged.
- The administration costs of these schemes are low relative to other forms of regulation.

Disadvantages

- There is the initial problem of assigning property rights.
- If a breach of property rights has occurred, there may be an expensive legal procedure to determine how much compensation should be paid and to whom.
- It may be difficult to agree on the monetary value of the external cost.

Now test yourself

TESTED

7 How can a system of tradable permits be used to reduce pollution?
8 Why might laws passed to reduce pollution fail to meet their objective?

Answers on p. 110

Government failure

Government failure arises as a result of government intervention in a market in an attempt to correct a market failure which causes output and consumption to move further away from the socially efficient output. In other words, government failure is a situation in which government intervention would result in a more inefficient allocation of resources and would, therefore, lead to a net welfare loss.

> **Government failure** is when government intervention results in a net welfare loss.

> **Typical mistake**
>
> Confusing government failure with market failure.

Causes of government failure

REVISED

Distortion of price signals

Government intervention often involves manipulation of prices, for example, by maximum or minimum price controls. However, such measures would undermine the key functions of the price mechanism such as signalling, rationing and incentives. Ultimately, this would mean that resources are not allocated efficiently.

Unintended consequences

Some types of government intervention may have an impact which was not predicted by policy makers. For example, high taxes imposed on spirits in the UK designed to raise tax revenues as well as preventing an increase in consumption actually resulted in a decrease in tax revenues. Similarly, very high taxes on cigarettes in the UK have resulted in a significant increase in cigarette smuggling from which the government gains no tax revenue.

Excessive administrative costs

Although government intervention might seem to be desirable, the costs may be considerable. For example, the cost of administering means-tested benefits may be very large.

Information gaps

When a government intervenes in a market it is unlikely to have all the information required. Consequently, the intervention could move output further away from the socially optimal level

> **Now test yourself**
>
> TESTED
>
> 9 Would government failure result in a movement closer to or further away from the socially efficient level of output?
> 10 How could government failure occur in the EU's system of fishing quotas?
>
> Answers on p. 110

Government failure in various markets

Government intervention in a market may have unforeseen and undesirable consequences. The following are examples where government failure might be observed:

● **Indirect taxes:** very high indirect taxes might result in smuggling as a means of avoiding the tax. Further, if the indirect tax is set too high it might result in a movement further away from the socially optimum level of output.

● **Agricultural stabilisation schemes**, e.g. minimum guaranteed prices. As explained previously, these schemes could result in massive surpluses which would involve huge storage costs. Further, such surpluses imply that resources may not be allocated efficiently. For example, in the case of wheat, it might suggest that land should be used for alternative crops.

● **Housing policies:** state provision of housing at low rents might be thought to be desirable for those on low incomes. However, housing subsidies prevent the market from working efficiently. For example, there will be little incentive for people to move even if their incomes rise so limiting the geographical mobility of labour.

● **Environmental policies:** subsidies have been given for the establishment of wind farms but many argue that the energy produced from them is relatively expensive and that they cause an environmental eyesore. A further example of government failure in this context was the payment by the government of £2.8 million to wind farm owners on one day in August 2014 to stop producing electricity because the electricity network was unable to cope with the amount of electricity being generated from this source.

These are just a few examples but there are many other examples including government intervention in the fishing industry which may result in the depletion of fish stocks; and high taxes on alcohol and tobacco which might encourage smuggling to such an extent that a further tax rise on these products could result in a fall in tax revenues.

Exam practice

1 (a) When a government increased the tax on whisky the tax revenue fell despite an increase in sales because there was increased tax evasion. This illustrates an example of:
   A   an inferior good
   B   asymmetric information
   C   external benefits
   D   government failure   [1]
  (b) Identify three possible sources of government failure.   [3]

2 (a) If a government provides a subsidy to producers of wind power, it will cause
   A   a decrease in consumers' surplus
   B   an increase in producer surplus
   C   a decrease in profits of producers
   D   an increase in external costs   [1]
  (b) In 2014, subsidies to wind farm owners were estimated to be £1.8 billion. The industry employs 15 500 workers.
   (i) Calculate the subsidy per worker to the wind farm industry in 2014.   [1]
   (ii) Explain one reason why subsidies are given to wind farm operators.   [2]

The price of raw sugar fell from 29 cents per pound in January 2011 to just 15 cents per pound in March 2015 following bumper crops and weak sales. Sugar has been associated with obesity, tooth decay and various health diseases such as diabetes. Consequently there has been pressure on manufacturers to reduce the amount of sugar in processed foods such as breakfast cereals and yoghurts. Meanwhile, consumers have increasingly been turning to sugar-free versions of products such as soft drinks. Such products are often sweetened with artificial sweeteners. However, for many people sugar is addictive: for example, they may be unable to drink tea or coffee without sugar and need frequent sugar boosts from biscuits, cakes and soft drinks. It has been estimated that a 10% rise in the price of sugar would only result in a 0.1% fall in the quantity demanded in the European Union.

Given the adverse health effects of excessive sugar consumption some scientists have proposed a tax of up to 100% on soft drinks and confectionery.

Sugar production often involves undesirable consequences. In Australia, for example, the expansion of sugar cane production has caused a number of problems such as drainage issues and disruption of habitats for wildlife. Further, production is increasingly dependent on the use of chemical fertilisers which has caused loss of fish, land erosion and a deterioration in the quality of the land.

Some local authorities in England pay for 3 free months' membership of a fitness club for people with high blood pressure and who are obese. If the person loses 10% of their body weight the free membership is extended for a further 3 months. The benefits of losing weight include lower blood pressure and a reduced risk of contracting other diseases such as diabetes. There are also benefits to the wider community, for example, higher productivity and less absenteeism by workers and lower costs incurred by the National Health Service.

(a) Calculate the price elasticity of demand for sugar from the information provided. Comment on your result. [4]

(b) What might be inferred about the cross elasticity of demand between sugar and artificial sweeteners? [5]

(c) Explain how producer surplus might be affected following the fall in demand for sugar. [6]

(d) Assess the reasons for the fall in the price of sugar. Illustrate your answer with a diagram. [10]

(e) Discuss whether a government decision to ban sugar production in the UK might result in government failure. [15]

EITHER

(f) Evaluate the case for a 100% tax on soft drinks and confectionery. [20]

OR

(g) Evaluate the private costs and external costs of sugar production. [20]

Answers and quick quizzes online

ONLINE

Summary

You should have an understanding of:
- Methods of providing public goods.
- Asymmetric information: meaning and significance.
- Ways of dealing with asymmetric information.
- Government failure: meaning and causes.
- Examples of government failure in different markets.

5 Measures of economic performance

Economic growth

Measuring growth

REVISED

Economic growth is a measure of an increase in **real** gross domestic product (GDP). GDP is the total amount of goods and services produced in a country in one year, or the total amount spent, or the total amount earned.

Potential economic growth is a measure of the increase in capacity in an economy. It can be shown by a movement outwards of the PPF curve (see chapter 1, page 12). It is a measure of how efficient the economy is in using its resources.

If an economy has two consecutive quarters (3 months, starting January, April, July or October) of negative economic growth then it is in a *recession*. The UK went into recession in 2008, and after a brief period of growth in 2010 and 2011 there was a return to recession in 2012. A recession means that there is less spending, income and output in the economy. It is likely to lead to firms closing, increased unemployment and a resulting fall in living standards.

> **Real** means that inflation has been taken into account. Real values are sometimes referred to as 'constant prices'. If inflation is left in the figures they are known as 'nominal' or 'current'.
>
> **Recession** — if an economy has two consecutive quarters of negative economic growth then it is in a recession. A quarter is 3 months, starting January, April, July or October.

Now test yourself

TESTED

1 What are the characteristics of a recession?

Answer on p. 110

Changing living standards

REVISED

An increase in GDP is likely to cause an increase in **standards of living**, which means that people can afford more goods and services, or feel that their lives are better because they do not need to work as hard to achieve their requirements in life.

However, a rising income does not necessarily make standards of living rise. It depends on how the extra money is distributed, whether inflation is being taken into account (real versus nominal), the amount spent on investment and long-term socially beneficial projects and population change. When the total population has changed (if there are more people then the increased income has to be spread out over the greater number) it is better to look at **GDP per capita**.

> **Standard of living** is a measure of the quality of life. The measure can include physical assets and consumption, and less easily measured variables such as happiness, lack of stress, length of hours worked, lack of pollution, capacity of houses.
>
> **GDP per capita** (per head) is total GDP divided by the population. Total population figures cannot be assumed to be constant when looking at GDP, so GDP per capita gives a better indicator of incomes.

Now test yourself

TESTED

2 Does a higher growth rate mean a country is enjoying higher living standards?

Answer on p. 110

Growth in different countries

An increase in GDP in one country of 10% does not mean that the country is doing better than a country with an increase of 5%. It depends on:

- how much of the output is self-consumed so does not appear as GDP
- methods of calculation and reliability of data
- relative exchange rates — do they represent the purchasing power of the local currency?
- type of spending by government — is money spent on warfare, or on **quality of life** issues such as education and health?

> **Quality of life** is a measure of living standards that takes into account more than just income (or GDP).

Volume versus value

An increase in the volume of output does not always mean that there is an increase in the value of output. Volume of output measures the number of items produced, but if these are falling in price (perhaps because lots of countries are producing the same thing) then value might fall even when volume rises.

> **Typical mistake**
>
> Economic growth is a change in the level of real GDP, not GDP itself. Do not give GDP figures on their own — show a percentage change.

> **Exam tip**
>
> Look out for 'falling growth levels'. If growth rates are falling but still above zero then *levels* of income are still rising, although at a slower rate.

Understanding purchasing power parities

Purchasing power parities (PPPs) are used to compare GDP in different countries, and take into account the cost of a 'basket of goods' that could be bought in each of the countries being compared. The PPP exchange rate is the rate where the basket of goods costs the same in each country.

> **Example**
>
> A Coldplay album costs £10 in the UK and $10 in the US. The exchange rate on the currency markets is £1 = $1.50 but the PPP rate is £1 = $1.
>
> This means the pound is overvalued (too strong) on the currency markets, and you would expect the official exchange rate of the UK economy to give values for incomes that are over-inflated in terms of purchasing power parity.

> **Purchasing power parities** — when values of income are expressed at PPP it means that the exchange rate used is the one where the same basket of goods in the country could be bought in the USA at this rate of currency exchange.

Gross national income (GNI) and gross national product (GNP)

Gross national income (GNI) measures income received by a country both domestically (gross domestic product) and net incomes from overseas.

Gross national product (GNP) is the total market value of all goods and services produced by domestic residents (gross domestic product) plus the value of output from sales abroad that residents have received, minus the value of output claimed by non-residents.

> **Exam tip**
>
> GNI is the same as GNP but from the point of view of income rather than output.

Exam tip

GNP may be much less than GDP if much of the income from a country's production flows to foreign people or firms. But, if the people or firms of a country hold large amounts of the stocks and bonds of firms or governments of other countries and receive income from them, GNP may be greater than GDP.

GNI and GNP measure output from the workers and companies of a particular nation, regardless of the country the income earners are based in.

National happiness

An alternative way to measure standards of living in a country is to use 'national happiness' which is a measure of national **wellbeing**. Surveys attempt to measure **subjective happiness**, such as friendship and social interactions, alongside the traditional measures such as real incomes.

> **Subjective happiness** is a measure of how people feel about themselves.

Now test yourself

TESTED

3 Assess one way in which happiness is considered more important than economic growth as an objective of government policy.

Answer on p. 110

Exam tip

Subjective happiness on any one day is an unreliable indicator, as our moods change with the weather, short-term health issues (such as headaches) or events in the news. So, for example, people might not be able to tell you accurately how they felt about life yesterday but if you keep on asking over several years they might be able to give you a good overall view.

Inflation

Inflation is a *sustained* rise in the *general* price level. It is a weighted average of spending of all households in a country (that is, general spending). Changes in the **consumer price index** (CPI) are used as the measure of inflation used for inflation targeting in the UK. The CPI does not include housing costs such as rent payments and mortgage interest repayments. Changes in the **retail price index** (RPI) (also known as the headline rate), include housing costs, and may be used in data for comparison with CPI.

> **Consumer price index** is the measure of inflation used for inflation targeting in the UK. It does not include housing costs such as mortgage interest repayments or rent.
>
> **Retail price index** is a measure of inflation. It is also known as the headline rate, and includes housing costs. The RPI is used for setting the state pension and for price capping (e.g. for stopping rail fares rising too quickly) so the RPI is an important measure. If housing costs rise faster than other components of inflation the RPI will be higher than the CPI.

Deflation is a fall in the general price level. It is a sign of stagnation in an economy. In recent years Italy has suffered from deflation.

Disinflation occurs when prices rise more slowly than they have done in the past. For example, inflation might fall from 3% to 2%, meaning that prices are rising but rising less quickly than they were. In 2015, falls in oil prices in the UK brought about disinflation, as inflation fell to 0.3% and beyond.

Exam tip

Deflation is a fall in the general level of prices. **Disinflation** is a fall in the rate of inflation, so prices are *rising more slowly*.

Exam tip

Look out for falling inflation levels. If inflation rates are falling but still above zero then *levels* of prices are still rising, although at a slower rate.

Now test yourself

TESTED

4 If oil prices go up sharply is this inflation?

Answer on p. 110

Calculating the rate of inflation

REVISED

Inflation is a measure of the increase in the average price level. The price level is measured by the consumer price index, which is a weighted average of things on which people spend their money. Key points to note:
- Inflation is measured in the UK by *changes* in the CPI.
- The CPI is given as an **index number**. This means that it is a number shown as a percentage relative to the **base year**, which is given the value 100.
- Inflation is usually shown on a year-to-year basis, so you need to calculate the change over the original × 100.

> **Typical mistake**
>
> What is inflation if the consumer price index changes from 125 to 130? This is an increase of (5/125) times 100 which is an inflation rate of 4% not 5%. Most people divide by 100 rather than the 'original', which is 125.

Households spend different amounts on various items. It is important to incorporate this in the calculation of inflation so that price changes will be fully reflected in the cost of living. In order to find a rate of inflation that represents the changes in costs of living that households experience:

- **Weights** are assigned to each item that is bought by the average household.
- The *Living Costs and Food Survey* collects information from a sample of nearly 7000 households in the UK using self-reported diaries of all purchases.
- The weights show the proportion of income spent on each item.
- A price survey is undertaken by civil servants who collect data once a month about changes in the price of the 650 most commonly used goods and services in a variety of retail outlets.

The price changes are multiplied by the weights to give a price index; you can measure inflation from this by calculating the percentage change in this index over consecutive years.

> An **index number** is a number shown relative to another number in percentage terms, so the actual figures are removed and just the relative difference is shown.
>
> A **base year** is used for comparison between price levels in different time periods. It is given the number 100.

> **Weights** show the proportion of income spent on items and are used to ensure that the percentage change in price reflects the impact on the average family in terms of their spending.

> **Exam tip**
>
> Many students think that the CPI or RPI is inflation. But it is *changes* in these price levels that show inflation.

Now test yourself

TESTED

5 Does the price survey involve looking at just 650 items? If more, why is this?

Answer on p. 111

The causes of inflation

REVISED

There are three main explanations of why inflation can occur:
- **Demand-pull inflation**. This occurs when aggregate demand (total demand) in the economy increases. It might be because interest rates

have fallen, the level of confidence has risen, governments might be spending more, or because exports are rising relative to imports. All of these changes will have multiplier effects (see page 91) which can cause upward pressure on prices.

- **Cost–push inflation.** This occurs when aggregate supply decreases, i.e. the total costs of production increase. This may be because oil prices have risen, the exchange rate has fallen (making imports more expensive) or because the minimum wage has risen in real terms.
- **Growth in the money supply.** Some economists (*monetarists*) argue that inflation is caused by increases in the money supply.

> **Demand–pull inflation** is caused by increases in **aggregate demand**. This means that spending is rising above sustainable levels. An example is that interest rates might be cut so that people want to spend more in the shops. More people wanting to buy the same amount of goods means that prices will rise.
>
> **Cost–push inflation** is inflation caused by decreases in **aggregate supply**. This means that costs of production are rising or firms are willing and able to produce less at any price level. For example, an increase in food prices will cause more general rises in costs in an economy.
>
> **Monetarism** is the school of economics based on the belief that inflation is always a problem of too much money in the economy.

> **Exam tip**
>
> A fall in the value of a currency can cause cost–push inflation (as imports become expensive) or cause demand–pull inflation (as exports become more attractive and imports become less attractive), so there is more total spending (aggregate demand) in the economy.

The effects of inflation

REVISED

Inflation is an important measure of the success of an economy, and inflation rates that are too high or too low are a sign that the economy is experiencing problems.

In the UK there is an **inflation target** (currently this is a 2% rise in CPI with a range allowed of + or −1%). This means that a rise in the average level of prices of 2% is the desired level.

If UK inflation is 2% then the average cost of living will rise by 2%. If earnings rise on average by 2%, then on average no one is worse off. But the measure of inflation might not be a true representation of the changes in living costs. It does not include housing costs, which are a significant item of expenditure for most households in the UK. Some people do not have representative spending patterns and so might experience cost of living rises of more or less than the average shown by the CPI.

Inflation is damaging to an economy for reasons including the following:
- Inflation above 3% may significantly damage **international competitiveness**, i.e. it makes exports relatively expensive in foreign markets and imports from abroad seem cheap. This tends to worsen the balance of payments.
- It is damaging for people on **fixed incomes**. If people find their incomes do not rise in **real terms** then they will get progressively worse off, even if in **nominal terms** they are earning the same amount or more.
- Inflation is damaging to workers if the rate of inflation is higher than their nominal wage rises. In this case, their real income is falling. However, if wages rise faster than inflation then real incomes rise.
- High inflation rates might make the Monetary Policy Committee decide on a rise in interest rates. This is known as **tight monetary policy**

> **Inflation target** — in the UK the government tasks the Monetary Policy Committee with the objective of 2% inflation, within a range of tolerance of plus or minus 1%.
>
> **International competitiveness** is the degree to which a country's goods and services can be sold on international markets.
>
> **Fixed incomes** — many groups of people, such as university students and pensioners, do not usually enjoy wage increases in line with inflation. This means that they suffer when the cost of living rises.
>
> **Real terms** are figures where inflation has been taken into account.
>
> **Tight monetary policy** is when the interest rates are kept high because of inflationary fears.

and can have damaging effects, for example on investment by firms (it falls because investment costs more), or for people paying off debts.

- Inflation can be damaging to the government because it makes it look as if it is unable to control the economy. But inflation is also good for governments if there are high levels of national debt. Debt does not change in its nominal value when there is inflation, so in real terms it is cheaper to finance and to pay back.

Now test yourself

TESTED ☐

6 How does a high inflation rate damage other parts of the economy?
7 Give two reasons why the CPI measure might be inaccurate as a measure of the average cost of living in the UK.
8 Cherry gets a 1% pay rise from her employer, but the rate of inflation is 4%. What, to the nearest whole number, happens to her real wage?

Answers on p. 111

> **Revision activity**
>
> Calculate your own rate of inflation, and that of the people with whom you live. Type 'inflation calculator' into a search engine, then type in the amount you spend on various items. The BBC and the statistics. gov.uk websites have very clear guidelines for this task.
>
> If you find your personal inflation rate is higher than average you might like to negotiate higher levels of pocket money.

> **Revision activity**
>
> Ask an older person who has had a mortgage whether the payments seemed to get smaller as they got older. If they found that it became easier to repay their mortgage this is because inflation eroded the real cost of financing it. It is the same benefit an indebted government gets when there is inflation.

Employment and unemployment

Employment

REVISED ☐

Employment can be measured as a level (number of people in work) or as a percentage (number of people in work divided by the total number of people who are **economically active** multiplied by 100).

Those people who are not available to work, such as students or people caring for other people as unpaid activity, people not of working age and those who are unable to work are referred to as **economically inactive**.

> **Typical mistake**
>
> Confusing economic activity with employment. This is incorrect, because people who are willing to work but cannot find employment are still economically active.

> **Economically active** — those people who are at work or who are willing to work. Also called the workforce, the term includes unemployed people.
>
> **Economically inactive** — those people who are not available to work, such as students or people caring for other people as unpaid activity, people not of working age and those who are unable to work.

Unemployment

REVISED ☐

Unemployment can be measured as a level (number of people looking for work but unable to find it) or as a percentage (number of people out of work divided by the total number of people who are economically active, multiplied by 100).

Types (or causes) of unemployment

- **Cyclical** (or demand-deficient) — where lack of spending in the economy/recession means that people are out of work. In a recession you expect this type of unemployment.
- **Structural** — where industries are in decline and workers' skills are becoming obsolete (out of date).
- **Frictional** — where people are between jobs.
- **Seasonal** — where people are out of work for some periods of the year, for example ski instructors in the summer and surf instructors in the winter.
- **Classical or real wage inflexibility** — where there are problems with the supply side of labour, e.g. the minimum wage is too high. This might be because the national minimum wage is set above the equilibrium wage. Some economists (classical approach) argue that this is the cause of persistent unemployment in some countries, and that the economy cannot be in equilibrium with demand deficiency.

Costs of unemployment

- Costs to the person without an income.
- Non-income costs to the unemployed person. Skills become obsolete, and people can lose confidence.
- Costs to firms — people don't spend as much in the shops.
- Costs to governments. Governments have to spend more on **jobseeker's allowance** (JSA) and they receive less in income tax and other taxes.

> **Jobseeker's allowance (JSA)** is a payment made to people who are willing and able to work but are not currently in employment. When an economy grows, JSA is likely to fall as more people who are willing to work do manage to find work.

Now test yourself
TESTED

9 If you add together the percentage of the population employed with the percentage unemployed you will only get to around 80% of the population in the UK. What is the other 20% doing?

Answer on p. 111

Measures of unemployment

The two measures of unemployment used in the UK are:
- The **ILO measure** (conducted by the Labour Force Survey): this uses a questionnaire to ask people aged 16–65 whether they have been out of work over the last 4 weeks and are ready to start within 2 weeks.
- The **claimant count:** this records people who are successfully claiming jobseeker's allowance.

Now test yourself
TESTED

10 Why might the ILO measure be higher than the claimant count measure?
11 Why might the claimant count rise relative to the ILO measure of unemployment?

Answers on p. 111

The distinction between unemployment and underemployment

Unemployed people don't have a job. But many people have jobs which don't offer them enough hours. These **underemployed** people are not taken into account in the unemployment figures, so the unemployment figures may under-represent the problem of joblessness. The Office for National Statistics (ONS) publishes figures for underemployment, and the figure is just over 10%. As an evaluation point you might consider that many people are also overqualified for the work they do, as well as wishing to work more hours or on a stable contract. For example, people on zero hours contracts might be able to take on more work if they could be sure it would be offered.

Significance of increased employment

The benefits of increased employment might include:
- **Increased incomes** — with rises in standards of living for households.
- **Improved skills (human capital)** of workers.
- **Multiplier effects** — as increased incomes lead to increased spending, so firms might see increased profits.
- **Higher government taxation revenue** as more people pay tax, and people spend more (VAT and corporation tax also tend to rise when employment rises).

> **Human capital** is the education and skills that a workforce possesses. Investment in people has a value.

Significance of decreased unemployment and inactivity

Many of the benefits are the same as the benefits of rising employment, but to these we can add:
- Falling government spending on JSA and other out-of-work benefits.
- Decreased unemployment can have exponential benefits because people who are out of the job market for a long period become increasingly unemployable.
- The job market becomes more flexible (there are more workers for employers to choose from).
- Decreased dependency ratios (the number of inactive people that active and employed people are supporting, directly or indirectly).

> **Revision activity**
>
> Using the reverse of the arguments for increasing employment, explain the costs of decreasing employment. Are these the same as the costs of increasing unemployment?

Migration and employment/unemployment

Migration may occur when people:
- are searching for work or better-paid work
- study abroad
- escape from social or political problems in original country
- accompany family members
- disagree with tax structures
- wish to 'get away from' or 'get to' people or places

The economic implications for employment and unemployment depend largely on the reasons for both **immigration** and **emigration**.
- If immigrants come into a country to fill vacancies, then immigration leads to an increase in employment.
- But if immigrants are looking for work and either do not find it or displace other people from work, then employment may be unchanged and unemployment might increase.

> **Migration** is a general term that looks at both immigration, emigration and the overall balance between the two in a country (net migration).
>
> **Immigration** is when people enter a country for long-term stay.
>
> **Emigration** is when people exit a country for long-term stay.

Typical mistake

Don't assume that migration means there is an overall cost to the government. Remember that employed immigrants pay tax to the UK government, increasing government revenue.

Now test yourself

TESTED

12 If immigrants come into the UK for full-time study, what will happen to the level of employment and unemployment?

Answer on p. 111

Balance of payments

The balance of payments is a record of international payments over the course of a year.

The current account

REVISED

The current account records payments for transactions between countries in the present year (other than investments or speculation) and comprises:

- trade in goods
- trade in services
- investment income (interest, profit and dividends)
- transfers, e.g. tax payments to foreign governments

Typical mistake

Thinking that investment income on the current account is the flow of investment funds, which are not featured on the current account. Investment income is the *reward* for investment, which is paid in the current period.

Exam tip

Capital account and financial account accounts relate to other parts of the balance of payments (investment and speculation) that you do not need to know for the AS exam, but you might see in some economics books. Be careful not to include anything other than the current account of the balance of payments in your AS revision notes.

Typical mistake

Thinking that imports are flow *in* rather than a flow *out* of money from a country. If you go on holiday in a foreign country then your spending is recorded as an import, because money is flowing out of the UK.

Current account deficit

REVISED

Causes of a **current account deficit** might include:

- the currency is too strong relative to other countries, e.g. if the pound buys many euros then people holding euros will not want to buy goods and services from the UK and people in the UK will be keen to buy things from the euro area

- high rates of inflation relative to other countries
- high wage costs relative to other countries
- high level of growth in a country, meaning people with higher incomes tend to buy more imports from abroad

> A **current account deficit** of the balance of payments occurs when more money is flowing out of the country than is flowing in.

Current account surplus

REVISED

Causes of a **current account surplus** might include:

- the currency is too weak relative to other countries, e.g. if the Chinese renminbi buys few US dollars then people in China will find it difficult to buy things from outside China
- low rates of inflation relative to other countries
- low wage costs relative to other countries
- low level of growth in a country, making it difficult to buy imports from abroad and creating a strong incentive for firms in the country to export

> A **current account surplus** on the balance of payments occurs when more money is flowing into the country than is flowing out.

The interconnectedness of economies through international trade

REVISED

International trade means that countries become interdependent, i.e. they rely on each other:

- for income (exports are part of a country's aggregate demand)
- for resources and goods and services (imports are necessary for production and consumption of goods in all countries)

Some people argue that interdependence is beneficial because it makes countries cooperate with each other, but it can also cause trade blocs to become powerful, which can leave some developing countries unable to trade fairly.

Revision activity

From the information given above, note down the causes of a current account surplus.

Now test yourself

TESTED

13 You go to Spain for a holiday. Is this an export or an import on the UK's balance of payments?

Answer on p. 111

Revision activity

Visit the BBC news website and find 'economy tracker'. Look at the measures of success of the UK economy according to these measures. Make a note of key figures such as the employment and unemployment rates, which you might refer to in your exam.

Exam practice

Changes to the composition of the basket of goods

Apple iPads and Samsung Galaxy tablets have been added to the basket of goods used to measure how quickly consumer prices are rising, as have teen novels, baby wipes and chicken and chips takeaways from fast-food outlets, according to the government body that compiles official inflation rates. The growing popularity of tablet devices made them suitable for addition in their own right for 2012. 'Chicken and chips' was being added because that type of product was under-represented, perhaps because cash-strapped Britons are consuming more cheap and easy meals at a time of high food prices.

The removal of prices for processing colour film reflects the growing use of digital cameras.

Source: adapted from The Office for National Statistics (ONS).

1 With reference to the article, explain why items get added and removed from the 'basket'. [5]
2 Examine the issue of what is in the 'basket' and the proportion spent on each item. [10]
3 Very few pensioners currently use tablet-device computers. Explain why this might cause a problem for a government in the process of setting the annual change in pension allowance. [6]

Answers and quick quizzes online

ONLINE

Summary

- Economic growth measures increases in real GDP or increases in potential capacity in an economy. It can lead to an increase in living standards, but this is not guaranteed, and many other factors are also required for an improvement in welfare.
- Controlling inflation is another of the main objectives of governments. In the UK there is a target for CPI changes of 2% + or −1%. The task of controlling inflation is the responsibility of the Monetary Policy Committee in the UK. It raises interest rates to try to cut inflation, and cuts interest rates if inflation is low to allow other areas of the economy to improve.
- Employment and unemployment are not opposites, but different ways of looking at efficiency in the use of the country's workforce. Inactivity helps to explain this. Underemployment is a good way of evaluating the measure of unemployment.
- The balance of payments is another way to judge the health of an economy, by looking at flows of money in and out of the country. Exports bring money flows into a country, and imports see money flowing out.

6 Aggregate demand (AD)

The characteristics of AD

Aggregate demand is made up of the following components (which are each explained in detail below):

consumption (C) + investment (I) + government expenditure (G) + net trade (exports (X) – imports (M))

AD is the total amount of planned spending on goods and services at any price level in an economy.

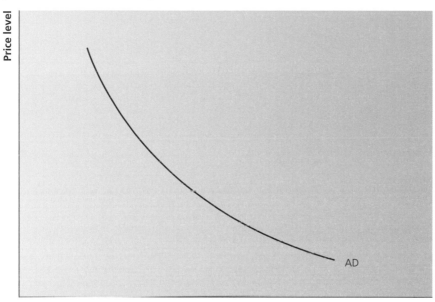

Figure 6.1 An aggregate demand curve

Important features about the aggregate demand curve:
- This diagram (see Figure 6.1) can be drawn as a straight line or a curve.
- Total expenditure by the economy remains much the same along the AD curve and this is called the **real balance effect**. This means that when prices fall, people still spend approximately the same amount in total but they buy a larger amount of items.
- Similarly, higher prices cannot be avoided by buying cheaper alternatives (which is the microeconomic analysis) so the total area under the AD curve remains approximately the same whatever the price level.

Revision activity

Give a reason why the AD curve is downward sloping. Remember that just saying 'prices are lower so we buy more' is not correct.

Exam tip

It does not make any difference to your mark whether you draw AD as a straight line or a curve. Choose the method that you feel most comfortable with.

The AD curve

A movement along the AD curve

- This occurs when there is a change in the price level caused by factors that are not related to aggregate demand, i.e. changes in aggregate supply.
- For example, a fall in oil prices (causing a decrease in the cost of production for all firms) would result in a expansion in AD and a fall in the price level, as shown in Figure 6.2.

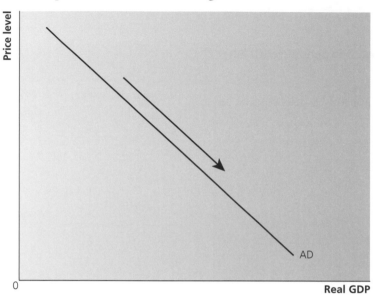

Figure 6.2 Expansion in aggregate demand

Shifts of the AD curve

Aggregate demand shifts when any one of the components C + I + G + (X − M) changes (see Figures 6.3 and 6.4). The analysis above explains why they might change. The size of the change depends on the multiplier effect (see page 91).

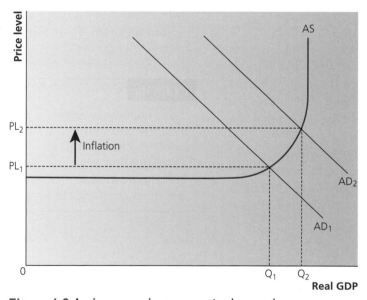

Figure 6.3 An increase in aggregate demand

Exam practice answers and quick quizzes at **www.hoddereducation.co.uk/myrevisionnotes**

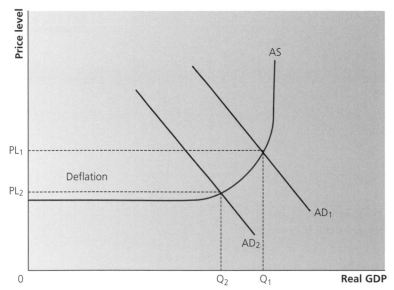

Figure 6.4 A decrease in aggregate demand

When aggregate demand shifts there will be changes in the price level and equilibrium real output.

- If aggregate demand increases, we expect the average level of prices to rise (inflation) and real output to increase (economic growth).
- If aggregate demand decreases, we expect the average level of prices to fall (deflation or falling prices) and real output to decrease (slowdown or recession).

Now test yourself

TESTED

1 What is the difference between a movement along the AD curve and a shift?

Answer on p. 111

Answer on p. 111

> **Exam tip**
>
> Remember to put the average price level or price level on the vertical axis of your diagrams. You will not gain the marks if you simply label it 'price' because this will look like a micro diagram. You should also avoid putting inflation on the vertical axis as this alters the analysis. On the horizontal axis never use 'Q' — use 'Real GDP' (or 'real national income') or another macro label such as this.

Consumption (C)

Consumption is spending by households on goods and services, and is the main component of AD (about 65%). For example, it records how much you spend on food and clothes. The main determinants of consumption are:

- **Interest rate (the cost of credit).** If **interest rates** rise, then it costs us more to borrow if we are going to spend on credit and it increases the opportunity cost of spending (i.e. saving); higher interest rates mean that more money can be earned by leaving money in the bank.
- **Consumer confidence.** If householders feel secure in their jobs and future prospects for the economy, then they are more likely to buy big-ticket items such as new cars or expensive electrical goods. Because of this, what people think is going to happen to the economy has a big influence on what actually does happen.
- **Wealth effects.** An increase in share or house prices means that households are willing and able to spend more. For example, if my house is worth more I might take out a larger loan on my house, and if my shares go up in value I might be more willing to book a foreign holiday, even if I do not in fact sell my house or my shares.
- **The level of employment.** The higher the level of employment the more will be spent in a country (which might lead to even higher employment).

> The **interest rate** is the cost of credit (borrowing) or the reward for saving.
>
> The **wealth effect** is the effect on spending or incomes when asset prices change.

Now test yourself

2 If interest rates fall what will happen to consumption?

Answer on p. 111

Investment (I)

Investment is defined as an increase in the capital stock. The main influences are:

- **The rate of economic growth.** If there is an increase in real GDP then firms will need more capital in order to meet the increased demand. So an increase in real GDP causes I to rise, and an increase in I causes real GDP to rise. This is a virtuous circle (unless it happens in reverse).
- **Confidence levels**. If firms think that they will sell more in the future (business confidence is high) they are more likely to invest today.
- **Interest rates**. If interest rates rise, investment tends to fall because it costs more to borrow the money in order to invest.
- **Animal spirits.** This is a term used by Keynes. Sometimes consumers and firms are not totally rational, and they act on gut instinct. According to Keynes, investment does not happen automatically — an additional boost might be needed by government. Firms might look at evidence that suggests that investment is worthwhile, but may need more than this to spur them into action. Consumers might decide they can afford to spend more but may need something to trigger the spending. Similarly, when prices and investment rise too quickly the government might need to intervene to calm down inflationary bubbles.
- **Risk**. The higher the level of risk, the lower the level of investment.
- **Access to credit.** Low interest rates do not necessarily mean that all firms can borrow cheaply. Banks might not be willing to take risks in their lending (even if the new financial controls allowed them to lend). In the aftermath of the credit crisis, firms often found it difficult to borrow even if they wanted to.
- **Government decisions**. Changes in government decisions and rules have a significant impact on capital spending, especially if firms have to face fines if they do not react. Government policy might mean changes in tax rates which directly affect firms. For example, if the government decides to cut **corporation tax** (a tax on profit) then firms are more likely to invest.
- **Government bureaucracy**. If the government relaxes planning restrictions — as they have done recently with buildings in the UK — firms are more likely to invest in building projects.

Gross investment is the total amount of investment, before any account is taken of depreciation of assets. Capital loses value as it wears out or becomes less efficient. Much investment in technology is quickly outdated, for example computer equipment.

Net investment takes account of the fall in value of capital assets. It is more useful as a sign of improvements in the prospects for the economy. It is the increase in capital less depreciation.

Corporation tax is a tax on profits that firms make. This tax affects the level of investment that firms make (aggregate demand) and it also affects the amount that firms are willing to supply at any price level, i.e. aggregate supply.

Government bureaucracy is the level of government regulations and paperwork that is required to make any business decisions.

Exam tip

Do not confuse interest rates with inflation. Interest rates may be used to control inflation, but otherwise they are very different concepts.

Government expenditure (G)

Governments can choose to some extent how much they spend and deliberately manipulate total spending in the economy by changing their own level of spending. This is called **discretionary fiscal policy**.

Points to note about government expenditure include:

- The government does not have to 'balance its books' in the short run, meaning that it can spend more or less than it earns in taxation.
- If the government spends *more* than it earns, this is known as a **fiscal or budget deficit**; this will increase the flow of income, or aggregate demand.
- If the government spends *less* than it earns, this is known as a **fiscal or budget surplus** and leads to a contraction of aggregate demand.
- The government automatically spends more in a recession as government spending increases on out-of-work benefits and taxation receipts fall as workers and firms earn less
- The government automatically spends less in a boom as government spending decreases and taxation receipts rise as wages and employment rise.

Many governments deliberately change taxes and benefits in order to influence the level of aggregate demand. For more on fiscal policy see chapter 10.

> **Fiscal policy** is the government's position or set of decisions on government spending and taxation.

> **Exam tip**
>
> Examiners tend to use the words 'budget' or 'fiscal' to mean the same thing, so do not be alarmed if you are asked to explain a budget or fiscal deficit — your answer will be the same. It means that the government is spending more than it is receiving in taxation.

Net trade (X – M)

Net trade (exports minus imports) is the last component of aggregate demand. In the UK this is a negative figure, meaning that the outflow of money for foreign goods and services is greater than the inflow that the UK receives from its exports.

The causes of changes in **net exports** are:

- **Real income.** If incomes rise within an economy, then there is a reduced incentive for domestic firms to export, because they can sell their goods and services in the domestic economy.
- **Change in exchange rate**. If the **exchange rate** rises, net exports are likely to fall as exports become less competitive and imports become more competitive in the domestic economy. However, in the short run a strong exchange rate might increase the value of exports and decrease the value of imports, as spending patterns do not adjust quickly to price changes. This is known as low price elasticity of demand for exports and imports. It causes the opposite reaction to AD than the one normally expected, as people take time to adjust their spending.
- **Changes in the state of the world economy.** The value of UK exports is heavily dependent on growth rates around the world. The slowdown in the Eurozone has caused UK exports to fall, especially to Spain. The crisis in the Eurozone has meant that spending on Chinese imports has been dramatically reduced, causing Chinese growth rates to fall because China is heavily dependent on exports to the Eurozone.
- **The degree of protectionism.** If there are high tariffs, quotas or other restrictions on trade, then firms will find it difficult to export to certain countries.
- **Non-price factors**. Demand for exports and imports is determined by many things apart from price, such as quality of engineering, reliability of after-sales service, tariffs and transport costs.

> **Net exports** — the export of goods and products means that money flows into a country; when the value of the money flowing out of the country (as imports) is deducted, a figure for net exports is the result.
>
> The **exchange rate** is the price of one currency in terms of another.

> **Exam tip**
>
> If our currency gets stronger, it means we can buy more of a foreign currency, so our imports are cheaper and exports cost more to people abroad. To remember this, use the mnemonic SPICED — 'strong pound, imports cheap, exports dear (expensive)'.

Now test yourself

3 Does a fall in the currency value increase or decrease aggregate demand?

Answer on p. 111

Exam practice

1 Which of the following is the best explanation of the shape of the AD curve?
   A When prices are lower people buy more.
   B When costs rise firms will raise prices.
   C When prices are lower the country is more likely to export and less likely to import.
   D When prices are higher the country is more likely to export and less likely to import. [1]
2 If interest rates rise, what is likely to happen to AD? Consider the impact on three components of AD. [6]

Answers and quick quizzes online

Summary

- Aggregate demand is the total amount of planned spending on goods and services at any price level in an economy. It is made up of C + I + G + (X – M).
- The largest component of AD in the UK, around two-thirds of AD, is consumption (C).
- Investment can be considered before it depreciates (gross investment) or after (net investment).
- Government spending is determined by the trade cycle. It is also determined by deliberate decisions of the government, set out in its fiscal policy or *budget*.
- Net trade is money received from exports (X) less money from imports (M). The overall impact is a major determinant of growth. In times of global recession, net trade will fall, meaning that the crisis in other countries (such as the south Eurozone area) will impact upon the UK.

7 Aggregate supply (AS)

The characteristics of AS

Aggregate supply is the amount that all firms in the economy are willing to supply at various price levels.

- It is based on the costs of production and incorporates rent, wages, interest and profits.
- As prices rise, firms are generally willing to supply more but there comes a point where firms reach maximum capacity which we will call full employment (at Y_f on Figure 7.1).
- You can draw AS as a straight line sloping upwards to indicate that there are rising costs as firms try to produce more.
- Or you can show AS with a horizontal section where there is spare capacity, an upward sloping part where there are bottlenecks in the economy, and a vertical part at full employment.

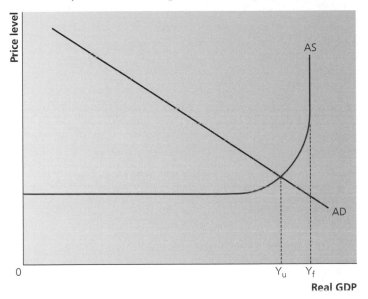

Figure 7.1 Aggregate supply

If the costs of production rise, the aggregate supply shifts up/left. For example:

- If the price of oil rises, firms will not be willing to supply unless they can receive more money for the same output.
- If investment falls, for example because interest rates have risen, then again aggregate supply decreases.
- If there is a shortage of certain factors of production, for example skilled labour, then this will raise costs for firms.

If an economy can increase output without significant increase in costs (that is, the aggregate supply is not vertical), we say there is **spare capacity** (or an output gap, see page 96). In this case, there are unused resources in the economy, meaning some unemployment (at Y_u in Figure 7.1).

> **Spare capacity** is where there are unemployed resources in an economy.

- The Keynesian view is that there can be equilibrium in an economy and also spare capacity.
- The argument is that you cannot leave unemployment and recession to disappear by themselves as market forces push prices down and make the resources more employable.

Approaches to aggregate supply

The **Keynesian approach** to aggregate supply reflects the belief that an economy can be at equilibrium when there is spare capacity.

The **classical approach** to aggregate supply reflects the view that if there is spare capacity in the economy it cannot be said to be at equilibrium, and eventually the spare capacity will disappear, i.e. the aggregate supply is vertical in the long run.

Movements along the aggregate supply curve occur when aggregate demand shifts and the price level changes (see Figures 7.2 and 7.3).
- If there is an increase in aggregate demand, aggregate supply will expand and firms will produce more (Keynesian AS).
- If there is a decrease in aggregate demand, aggregate supply will contract and firms will produce less (Keynesian AS).

> The **Keynesian approach** is the view that there can be equilibrium unemployment, and governments can take action to stimulate aggregate demand to achieve long-term growth and employment.
>
> The **classical approach** is the view that markets work best if left to themselves. If there is unemployment, then labour markets should be left to themselves. Wages will fall until people can find work.

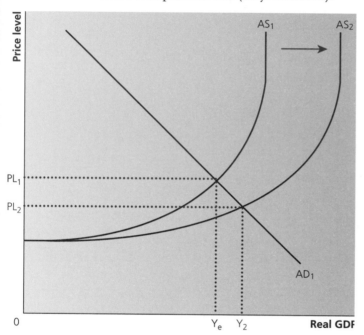

Figure 7.2 An increase in aggregate supply

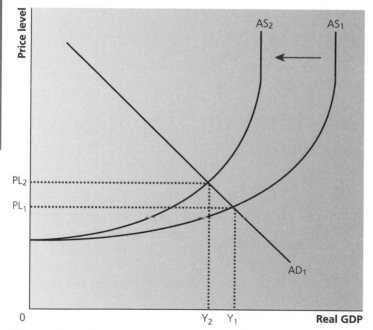

Figure 7.3 A decrease in aggregate supply

> **Exam tip**
>
> It is probably worth drawing the AS curve as a curve rather than a straight line. This will make it easier for you to talk about output gaps and other Keynesian analysis. It will also make it easier for you to evaluate, as you can discuss where the AD crosses the AS and the differing impact of the price level on real output that results.

Exam practice answers and quick quizzes at **www.hoddereducation.co.uk/myrevisionnotes**

Now test yourself TESTED

1 Why do AS curves sometimes get drawn as a backwards-facing L-shape?

Answer on p. 111

Why does aggregate supply shift? REVISED

There are many changes that might make firms willing to supply more or less at any given price level. If costs to firms decrease, we say that there is an increase in aggregate supply, and if costs to firms increase, we say that there is a decrease in aggregate supply.

Short-run AS

The following factors might cause a shift in aggregate supply in the **short run**:

- **Change in costs of raw materials.** If the cost of oil rises, the cost of production of almost everything will rise, meaning that aggregate supply decreases (shifts to the left or upwards).
- **Change in the level of international trade**. If, for example, trade is inhibited by a new tax on imports (a tariff), costs for domestic firms tend to rise as they cannot enjoy low production costs using cheap raw materials.
- **Change in exchange rates.** If the pound gets stronger, imports become cheaper and aggregate supply increases.
- **Change in tax rates.** If there is a cut in an indirect tax such as VAT you would expect AS to increase.

These changes mean that firms have a change in their costs of production, but no change in the total amount they are able and willing to make, i.e. their productive capacity remains the same.

Long-run AS

The following factors might cause a shift in aggregate supply in the **long run**.

- **Technological advances.** New computer-aided technology, for example, can reduce costs for a broad range of firms.
- **Relative productivity changes.** Productivity is defined as output per unit of input. If there is an improvement in the division and workflow becomes more efficient, then AS shifts down or to the right.
- **Education and skills changes.** If more people are well educated then aggregate supply increases.
- **Demographic changes and migration.** Demographic changes are the changes in the way the population is made up, e.g. when people live longer and the birth rate also falls we will see an ageing population. Demographic changes have a direct effect on the supply, skills and cost of labour, and therefore impact on aggregate supply as a whole. Migration has a specific demographic effect in that many migrants are of working age or are still students, so increases in migration in the short run cause the aggregate supply to increase, but if migrants stay in the country and have children or become dependent in their old age, the effect on aggregate supply might stagnate.

- **Competition policy and regulation changes.** If firms are forced to compete with each other rather than act as monopolies, they have to cut prices or improve their quality. Effective policing of competition makes the aggregate supply increase (shift right or down). If the government makes new laws to make it easier to set up and run businesses, then aggregate supply increases. This is sometimes called a cut in red tape or cut in bureaucracy. Some regulations add to firms' costs (a decrease in AS).
- **Changes in the minimum wage.** Increases in the minimum wage can increase costs for firms meaning that aggregate supply falls. However, there is evidence that increasing minimum wages can increase productivity of workers, which might mean that aggregate supply increases.
- **Changes in the tax and benefit system.** A cut in taxes on firms might increase aggregate supply. A cut in benefits might make people more desperate to keep their jobs or to find work, meaning productivity increases — although it might mean that people are less healthy, or less able to concentrate at work, or cause living standards to worsen.

These changes mean there is a change in the productive capacity of an economy, or that the economy can produce more at any given price level.

Now test yourself

 TESTED ☐

2 Will an increase in the interest rate cause aggregate supply to increase or decrease?

Answer on p. 111

> **Exam tip**
>
> When you are trying to decide whether there will be a change in AD or AS, remember that AS is the firms' perspective. Think about costs of production.

> **Typical mistake**
>
> Shifting AS the wrong way. Remember than an increase in AS makes it shift right or down. This sounds a bit odd. But it is because when there is an increase, it is the *output* increasing at any particular price level.

Exam practice

1 Explain the difference between production and productivity. [2]
2 Using a Keynesian long-run AS curve, annotate the diagram below to show the effect of a **decrease** in productive capacity on an economy where there is a negative output gap. [2]

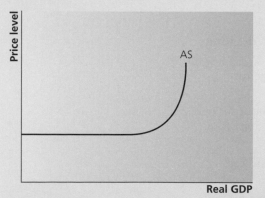

3 There is a rise in exchange rates. This means that aggregate supply will:
   A   increase in the short run (shift downwards/right) but not change in the long run
   B   increase in the short run (shift downwards/right) and may increase in the long run
   C   decrease in the short run (shift downwards/right) but not change in the long run
   D   not change in the short run (shift downwards/right) but decrease in the long run [1]

Answers and quick quizzes online

ONLINE ☐

Summary

- Aggregate supply is the amount that all firms in the economy are willing to supply at various price levels.
- When the price level changes there is a movement along the AS curve. This occurs because there has been a change in aggregate demand. AS expands when AD increases, and contracts when AD decreases.
- Aggregate supply shifts when costs that firms face change, or the amount they can produce at any particular price changes.
- Short-run changes in aggregate supply occur when costs change. Examples are changes in oil prices, exchange rates or taxes.
- Long-run changes in aggregate supply occur when output capacity changes. Examples are changes in the quality of factors of production or improved competition.

7 Aggregate supply (AS)

8 National income

The concept

National income is the amount received by various agents in an economy, by households, firms and government.

- It is the same as gross domestic product (GDP) measured by households, firms and government.
- It is the same as total spending by households, firms and government.
- It is the same as gross domestic income, which is all the income earned in the economy.
- This assumes that **leakages** (savings, tax and imports) and injections (investment, government spending and exports) have been taken into account.

National income is a flow of money, i.e. a movement of money from one person to another, rather than a stock of money such as savings in a bank, physical **assets** such as buildings or shares. The stock of assets in an economy is called **wealth**.

> **Leakages** (also known as 'withdrawal') are an exit from the circular flow of money. These comprise saving, taxation and the money spent on imports.

> An **asset** is an accumulation of wealth; factors which can be used to provide income in the future.
>
> **Wealth** is a stock of assets, e.g. factories or land.

Income and wealth

REVISED

There is a strong **correlation** between **income** and wealth. The ownership of wealth in itself can mean that there are interest payments or rent. When wealth changes in value, e.g. house prices rise or fall, there is an impact on people's spending and therefore incomes. For example, if my house is worth more than I paid for it, I might feel more confident about buying a new car and the bank manager might lend me the money because he is confident that my house can act as **collateral**.

> **Income** is a flow of money, e.g. wages.
>
> **Collateral** assets are used as security for a loan.

Injections and withdrawals

Injections

REVISED

Changes to the flow of income (see Figure 8.1) occur when there is a change in one of the three **injections** into the circular flow of income.

> **Injections** are an input into the circular flow of money. These inputs comprise investment, government spending and export income.

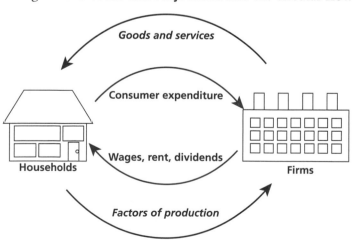

Figure 8.1 The circular flow of income (income is shown in red)

The injections are:

- **Investment (I):** an increase in the capital stock (assets).
- **Government spending (G):** where the government buys goods and services such as health care in the NHS.
- **Exports (X):** where people from abroad buy domestically produced goods and services.

Investment is an increase in spending when capital assets are bought as well as consumer items. So, for example, if a firm buys a new machine, there is more spending in the economy because the machine has to be made, which in turn means a greater number of incomes.

> **Typical mistake**
>
> Confusing saving with investment. In fact, they are complete opposites. Saving represents a decrease in the amount of spending in the economy as we forgo current spending for future spending.

Withdrawals

REVISED

Withdrawals are leakages out of the circular flow of income. If money is not re-spent within the economy, then it is being withdrawn or pulled out of the circular flow. The three reasons this happens are:

- **Savings (S).** When we decide to spend money later rather than now it means that there is less spending in the current time period.
- **Tax (T).** When the government demands your money you cannot spend it. It is true that in many cases all the money that the government takes in tax is re-spent as government spending (G), but if the government starts to run a budget surplus, then this will not be the case. Try to think of G and T as independent.
- **Imports (M).** When we buy goods and services from abroad, our money or spending flows out of the country. This means less income for the domestic circular flow.

Now test yourself

TESTED

1 If the government decreases its spending on defence, what will happen to the total amount of spending in an economy?

Answer on p. 111

Equilibrium levels of real national output

Equilibrium

REVISED

When aggregate demand meets aggregate supply there is an **equilibrium** point, which tells us the price level and real GDP of a country (see Figure 8.2).

> An **equilibrium** is a balancing point where there is no tendency to change.

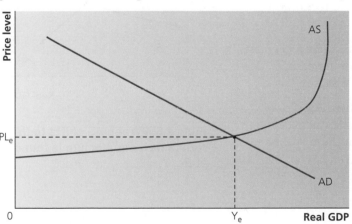

Figure 8.2 Equilibrium

An equilibrium is a balancing point where there is no tendency to change the price level or output level.

● If prices were higher than the balancing point PL_e, there would be a tendency for them to fall because supply would be greater than demand and there would be lots of unsold goods and services.
● If prices were lower than the balancing point, there would be shortages and prices would start to rise in order to make sure that everyone could get what they were prepared to pay for.
● If, for example, a worldwide recession and a fall in aggregate demand occurred, you would expect to see falls in prices (or that prices would not rise very quickly).

The use of AD/AS diagrams to show how shifts in AD or AS cause changes in inflation and growth

REVISED

When AD shifts to the right (expansionary) then we would expect there to be an increase in the equilibrium price level, i.e. inflation, and an increase in growth, i.e. an increase in real national output. This is shown in Figure 8.3.

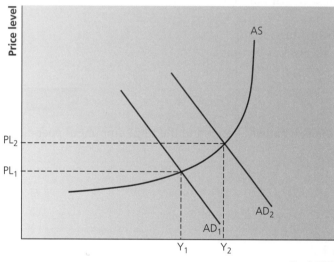

Figure 8.3 When AD shifts to the right a new equilibrium is found at $PL_2 Y_2$

However, this depends on AS being upward sloping. The more elastic the AS, the more the effect is seen on the growth axis rather than the price level axis. If AS is perfectly inelastic (the classical approach discussed on p. 84), then there will be no effect on output at all, and just an increase in prices.

When AS shifts to the right we would expect there to be a decrease in the equilibrium price level, i.e. deflation, and an increase in growth, i.e. an increase in real national output. See Figure 8.4.

However, this depends on AD crossing the AS where AS is not perfectly elastic (horizontal). If AS is perfectly elastic (the Keynesian output gap approach discussed on pp. 83–84), then there will be no effect on output or prices at all. The only effect would be an increase in the **output gap**.

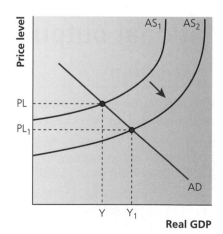

Figure 8.4 When AS shifts to the right a new equilibrium is found at $PL_1 Y_1$

Now test yourself

TESTED

2 Is equilibrium a good thing?

Answer on p. 112

The multiplier

The multiplier ratio

REVISED

The multiplier shows the amount by which a change in an injection or leakage causes total spending to change. It is the result of income being re-spent in the economy, having second and successive effects. The multiplier ratio, if written as x:y, shows how much of an impact an initial injection (x) will have on total incomes (y).

If the injections into the circular flow increase, then there will be a larger final change on total spending in the economy. The multiplier times the injection gives the final change to spending.

If the leakages from the circular flow increase, then the multiplier effect will be smaller. For example, when the 2008 recession hit the UK, the saving ratio rose markedly, reducing the multiplier effect.

Understanding marginal propensities (the tendency to do something with any extra money you have)

REVISED

- If I give you £10 and you spend half of it straight away, then you have a marginal propensity to consume (MPC) of 0.5, that is, 50% of any extra injection will be re-spent in the economy in macroeconomic terms. The MPC is 0.5.
- If I give you £10 and you save £1, then your marginal propensity to save (MPS) is 0.1. The more you save, the less you spend, so the lower the multiplier is. This means that an injection has a smaller overall impact on the economy. The multiplier ratio falls when the marginal propensity to save rises.
- If I give you £10 and you buy some cigarettes, which have a specific tax of £3, then the effect on the economy will not be as great as if you spent the money on some locally grown apples (no tax). The higher the marginal propensity to tax (MPT), the lower the multiplier ratio.
- If I give you £10 and you spend the money at Starbucks, the profits will leave the country as an import on the current account (investment income). So, if £1 leaves the country to return to the USA, the marginal propensity to import (MPM) is 0.1, and the effect is to reduce the value of the multiplier compared to buying some milk produced by UK cows.

The multiplier is 1 divided by the sum of the marginal propensities to withdraw. In other words, it is an inverse relation to the amount I end up spending in my own economy, that is $1/(1 - \text{MPC})$ or 1 divided by what is left when everything else has leaked out of the circular flow of income.

The multiplier process

For your exam you need to be able to show the effect of the multiplier numerically. Every time AD shifts or there is a change in an injection into the circular flow you should mention the multiplier. So for example, for any extra £1 that is injected into the circular flow, 0.1 or 10% might be saved (the marginal propensity to save or MPS), 0.4 or 40% might be spent on tax (marginal propensity to tax or MPT), 0.4 or 40% might be spent on imports (marginal propensity to import or MPM). All that is left is 0.1 or 10%, which is the amount that will be re-spent within the economy (the marginal propensity to consume or MPC).

Using these numbers we can say that the multiplier is 1/(MPS + MPT + MPM). This means that the effect on the economy of a new injection will have a magnified impact on the total expenditure in the economy, but this is limited by the amount of money that *leaks out* of the circular flow. Put another way, the multiplier is 1/(1 − MPC) meaning that the increase in total spending depends on how much is left for spending in the economy when all the leakages have been taken out.

Now test yourself

3 If there is an injection of £1 million into an economy and the multiplier is 2, what is the total change in spending in the economy?

Answer on p. 112

The effects of the economy on the multiplier

The changes in the economy, such as recession or boom, stock market bubbles, crashes or the fear of unemployment or rising house prices, can have a significant impact on the multiplier. For example, if house prices rise people tend to feel much more confident about spending and less worried about saving. This makes the multiplier rise. By contrast, in a credit crisis and economic recession the multiplier is likely to fall as people start to save more in case something awful happens. In 2009 savings rose significantly in many developed countries.

Calculations using the multiplier

If the multiplier is given, then you simply multiply the number given with the change in the injection to give the total overall change in national income.

So, for example, if the multiplier is 2 in the UK and there is an increase of £10 billion through exports to Singapore, then the total change in national income is £20 billion. If, however, the multiplier is 2 and there is a fall in national income through a cut in investment of £2 billion, then the total fall in national income is £4 billion.

Sometimes you might be asked to show the change that the injection will trigger, not the overall change. To do this, just take off the initial change in the injection. For example, if the multiplier is 2 in the UK and there is an increase of £10 billion through exports to Singapore, then further change in national income is £10 billion.

Another calculation you might need is to work out the value of the multiplier itself. For example, assume the multiplier is 2. If there is a rise in the marginal propensity to save, from 0.1 to 0.2, the multiplier will go from 1/0.5 to 1/0.6 = 1.67. So an increase in saving means that the multiplier falls in value. This means that any change in an injection will have a smaller impact on the overall level of spending.

The significance of the multiplier to shifts in aggregate demand

REVISED

If there is a change in any one of the injections or leakages, the total effect on the economy as a whole will be greater than the original change as long as it is above 1. The multiplier magnifies the impact of changes on the economy as a whole — the larger the multiplier, the greater the impact of any changes in injections or leakages. Every time you shift aggregate demand (AD) you must remember to shift it that bit further because of the multiplier. The bigger the multiplier ratio, the larger the overall AD shift. Remember that this can be a magnified increase or a magnified decrease.

Exam practice

1 In 2015 the Bank of England estimated that the marginal propensity to import in the UK rose from 0.2 to 0.3.
   (a) Define the term 'marginal propensity to import'. [1]
   (b) If the value of the multiplier was 1.25 before the change, calculate the new value of the multiplier, if everything else is unchanged. [2]
   (c) Which one of the following is the most likely cause of the rise in the marginal propensity to import?
      A a recession in the UK
      B an increase in underemployment
      C a fall in the interest rate
      D a rise in the exchange rate [1]
2 Discuss the likely impact on aggregate demand when there is an increase in the value of the currency. [20]

Exam tip

Note that for an AS exam you choose from two essay titles, and these are worth 20 marks.

Answers and quick quizzes online

ONLINE

Summary

- The main piece of analysis in macroeconomics, and the building block for most of the conclusions you will need to reach, can be found in aggregate demand and supply analysis.
- **Aggregate demand:** there are forces which determine how much people in an economy are prepared to buy at any price level, and the agents of this demand are consumers, firms, the government and foreign purchasers of our exports. We take off the value of imports and use the formula AD = C + I + G + (X – M).
- **Aggregate supply:** the amount that firms are willing to supply at any price level. The higher the prices that can be charged, the more

firms are willing to supply. The curve shifts when there are changes in costs that affect all firms, such as changes in oil prices, taxes or productivity of workers.
- Putting aggregate demand and supply together we get an equilibrium price level and output, which tells us what inflation and growth will be as AS or AD shifts. You will be examined on the causes of these shifts — remember that changes in determinants of aggregate demand are magnified by the working of the multiplier. This is the impact of incomes being re-spent in an economy, so any change in spending has second and subsequent round effects.

9 Economic growth

Causes of growth

Growth occurs when there is an increase in aggregate demand or aggregate supply, meaning that there is a new equilibrium output at a level where more is produced.

- It occurs with multiplier effects when there is a shift in aggregate demand.
- If the aggregate supply curve is vertical then when aggregate demand shifts there will *not* be growth — in other words, actual growth cannot occur beyond full capacity.

Aggregate demand shifts

Aggregate demand increases when something causes any of the components to increase. Below is a list of possible causes of increases.

Increase in consumption (C)

- A cut in the interest rate means the opportunity cost of saving falls, and the cost of borrowing to invest falls. It can also lead to falls in the cost of mortgage interest repayments, so people have more money left to spend on other things in the economy.
- Increase in confidence.
- Wealth effects from rising house or share prices.

> **Typical mistake**
>
> Consumption is a measure of the spending on goods and services in an economy. It is neither an injection nor a leakage, but a measure of the flow of income in an economy.

Increase in investment (I)

- Firms invest more when the cost of borrowing falls (interest rate cut).
- Increase in confidence of firms. If firms think there will be growth they are more likely to invest, which in itself is likely to stimulate growth.

> **Typical mistake**
>
> Investment is *not* saving in a bank. Investment is an increase in capital assets, for example buying a machine.

Increase in government spending (G)

Governments can use fiscal policy to stimulate the economy. This means spending on government projects, such as road building and education, when the rest of the economy is lacking in aggregate demand. Note that this is a Keynesian policy and that classical economists argue that it will only cause inflation or debt.

Increase in net exports (X – M)

Economies can be stimulated through export-led growth. China and Germany notably sailed through the last recession by maintaining spending through exports. In order to stimulate exports, the following strategies might be successful:

- Hold the exchange rate down (as in China holding the renminbi down). This makes exports relatively cheap and imports relatively expensive. However, in the UK we have a fully floating exchange rate and no manipulation is possible.

- Reduce tariffs and quotas. Encouraging trade tends to lead to an improvement in exports in the long run, but the initial effect is often an increase in imports, which actually reduces AD.
- Encourage the productivity and efficiency in export markets. The problem is that this is really a supply-side policy but it has an impact on the aggregate demand side.

> **Exam tip**
>
> International trade is very important for economic growth because an increase in exports or fall in imports will make AD shift to the right, with **multiplier effects**. Export-led growth means that the economy can grow without a worsening of the current account of the balance of payments.

> **Typical mistake**
>
> Getting confused about the impact of imports on aggregate demand. Remember that when a country imports goods, money is flowing out, so a rise in imports means that more money is leaving the country. This means there is less spending within this country, so there is a fall in aggregate demand.

Aggregate supply shifts

REVISED

Shifting AS to the right or down comes under the category of supply-side policies. These tend to be long run and involve enabling firms to produce more at lower costs. The policies used to achieve this are covered in the section on supply-side policies in chapter 10, p. 103.

> ### Now test yourself
>
> TESTED
>
> 1 What happens to growth if there is an increase in investment?
>
> **Answer on p. 112**

Economic growth – actual and potential

REVISED

Economists have two very different meanings for the term 'economic growth':

1 **Actual growth** is the measure of changes in **real GDP**, found by adding up all the incomes in the country, or all the spending, or all the output. Although none of these measures is entirely reliable, between them we can get a good indication of the changes of activity in the economy.

2 **Potential growth**, probably a more important measure than actual growth, shows how much the economy could produce if all the resources were being used. It is useful for measuring the success of governments and assessing the likelihood of changes in living standards over time.

> **Actual growth** is the increase in real GDP.
>
> **Real GDP** is the output of an economy, with the effects of inflation removed.

The difference between the actual and potential growth is the **output gap**, and the bigger the output gap, the more inefficient the economy is in its use of resources. In fact a persistent output gap tends to lead to a fall in potential output.

Sustainable growth is the highest rate of growth which does not compromise the welfare of future generations. For example, if an economy grows very quickly by mining all its resources, it might find it difficult to grow in the future.

> **Potential growth** is the amount by which a country could increase its production if all resources were used efficiently.
>
> The **output gap** is the difference between actual GDP (or growth) and potential GDP (or growth).

Output gaps

Output gaps are a sign that the country is not using its resources efficiently, or at their maximum potential. They are formed for a variety of reasons:

- resources available are not suited to the needs of the economy
- the welfare system pays generously for some people not to work
- the effects of relocation of production to other countries
- increased competitiveness of other countries
- structural changes, meaning the economy no longer produces output that is tailored to the needs of the market, e.g. ship-building when the government decides to cut back on the size of the navy.

A negative output gap exists when actual growth rates are below potential growth rates. This is shown in Figure 9.1 by the distance Y_1 to Y_{FE}. Keynesians believe these can persist in the long run.

Revision activity

The Office of Budget Responsibility (OBR) (budgetresponsibility.org.uk) makes a regular estimate of the size of the output gap. Find out what it is today, according to its measure. Does the OBR have any doubts about the reliability of its own measure?

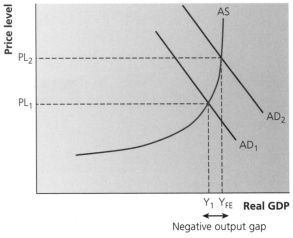

Y_{FE} is employment real output

Figure 9.1 Negative output gap using a Keynesian AS curve

A positive output gap is when growth rates are higher than the economy can sustain. This can be shown on a classical AS curve, as a temporary situation where the economy can produce more, but this cannot be sustained in the long run. In the long run, the AS is vertical and the positive output gap disappears. This is shown in Figure 9.2.

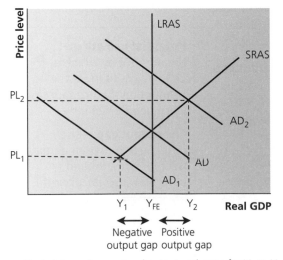

Y_{FE} is full employment real output and same for Y_2 to Y_{FE}

Figure 9.2 Positive and negative output gaps

Exam practice answers and quick quizzes at **www.hoddereducation.co.uk/myrevisionnotes**

It is difficult to measure both positive and negative output gaps, because we cannot tell what the level of potential output is. All we know is actual output (as measured by real GDP). The potential level depends on spare capacity, and without actually trying to use the spare capacity, we do not know how much the economy can produce.

Typical mistake

Thinking that a falling rate of growth means that real GDP is falling. If the rate of growth is still positive, then a falling rate means that incomes are rising, albeit more slowly.

Now test yourself

TESTED

2 If growth rates change from 3.2% to 2.0%, what has happened to the level of real GDP?

Answer on p. 112

Exam tip

There are many ways to draw an output gap on a diagram. Make sure that you are confident in at least one of these ways, e.g. drawing a PPF curve where the point of output is not on the PPF but inside the curve.

Trade (business) cycle

Economic growth changes at different speeds, and there is a pattern that can be observed over time, usually 7 to 10 years. The pattern can involve a **boom** (rapid economic growth) and a **slump** (very slow growth) or even a **recession** (two consecutive quarters of negative economic growth, as in many countries in 2008). Between the boom and the slump there is a slowdown, and between the slump and the boom there is a recovery.

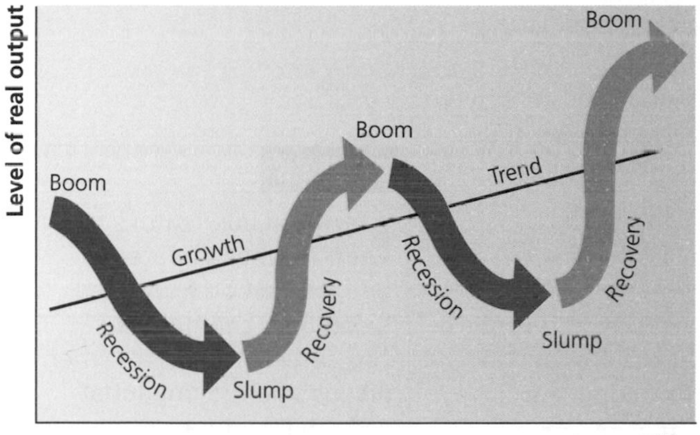

Figure 9.3 The economic cycle

Characteristics of a boom

REVISED

In a boom there is often high employment, increasing living standards, increased investment, but sometimes inflation, widening inequality and increased negative externalities (see The impact of economic growth, p. 98).

Characteristics of a recession

REVISED

In a recession there is often high unemployment or underemployment, lower or not increasing living standards, but sometimes lower inflation, narrowing inequality and decreased negative externalities.

The absence of causes of growth (or constraints on growth) are useful as an evaluation tool when trying to explain a recession. The following are other factors which might be used:

- lack of **investment** funds or cash to run businesses
- weak or obstructive governments
- currency instability or a **fixed exchange rate** or too-high exchange rates.

Investment is an increase in the capital stock.

A **fixed exchange rate** is when governments prevent their currencies from moving with market forces. This can be achieved by legislation or through buying and selling currencies to maintain a certain rate.

- lack of human capital
- lack of access to international trade, or a high level of **tariffs** and other forms of protectionism

> A **tariff** is a tax on imports that can prevent growth if it means that firms cannot acquire raw materials or capital goods.

Now test yourself

TESTED ▢

3 Why can high exchange rates be viewed as a constraint on growth?

Answer on p. 112

The impact of economic growth

Benefits of growth

REVISED ▢

- **Increased incomes and standards of living.** Total income for the country is increasing when there is economic growth, and as long as inflation is not increasing at the same rate at least some people will be better off. However, the distribution of income is likely to change, and while some people might not be any better off, the gap between them and others might increase.
- **Firms are likely to experience increased profits** when there is increased growth. This is likely to mean that they can make more profits and shareholders can enjoy increased returns. However, firms making inferior goods, i.e. where demand falls for these goods when income rises, are likely to suffer. For example, lower-end food suppliers and pound shops tend to do less well in a period of economic growth.
- **Governments benefit in a boom** because more people are working and paying tax and fewer people need benefits such as jobseeker's allowance (JSA), so there is likely to be a fiscal improvement in a boom. However, many governments see a period of economic growth as a time to reduce income inequalities, which become more apparent as top-end incomes tend to rise faster, so rates of benefits such as pensions increase.
- **Current and future living standards.** Growth lifts people out of poverty, and can provide many opportunities for an economy. Developing countries can gain foreign investment, foreign currencies can flow into an economy, and there are likely to be improvements in infrastructure of all types, from airports to mobile phone coverage.

> **Exam tip**
>
> Inferior goods feature in Theme 1 (see chapter 2) and will not be examined directly in Theme 2, but you can refer to them when discussing the impact of growth on some companies where demand falls when consumers have increased income.

Costs of growth

REVISED ▢

Damage to the environment

Damage to the environment can occur, for example, through increased carbon emissions. The by-product of most industrial production is CO_2 and this has an impact on the ozone layer, acid rain and causes health problems such as asthma. Growth also causes a rise in fuel emissions (because a greater number of people are travelling to work or travelling to a holiday destination, possibly further away or more often).

Evaluation: higher incomes can in fact mean that there is more money to clear up environmental damage: catalytic converters can be fitted to cars; firms can be forced to use a certain percentage of bio-fuels or renewable energy; there is money available for investment in new machinery; and firms and governments can be compelled to adopt carbon-offset schemes, or invest in 'green' technology.

Exam practice answers and quick quizzes at www.hoddereducation.co.uk/myrevisionnotes

Balance of payments problems

Higher incomes mean that people can afford to import more, and the need of firms to export is no longer so pressing as higher profit margins can be made through selling at home rather than abroad. So X falls, M rises and the balance of payments worsens.

Evaluation: if growth is caused by increasing exports however, then an improvement of the balance of payments is expected. For example, in 2015 Germany had the highest rate of growth in the EU, but also a balance of payments surplus.

Exam tip

Remember that an increase in income makes individuals and firms better off, but the country as a whole is worse off if the extra income is used to buy more from abroad.

Widening income distribution

The **distribution of income** is a measure of the difference in incomes between different groups in an economy. These groups can be measured in a variety of ways, but one common way is to compare the highest **decile** or 10% of income earners with the lowest decile.

A **decile** is a 10% chunk of an ordered set of data.

When the economy grows, those who reap the benefits tend to be those who already have a good job. For example, the manager or shareholders of a business will enjoy the increased profits, whereas other employees, e.g. cleaners or factory workers, are not likely to see dividends which relate to profits.

Evaluation: with continued growth, workers may lobby for higher incomes and the rewards may trickle down to those on the lower rungs of the pay scale, especially if there is a shortage of labour and these workers cannot be replaced by machinery. The higher the appropriate skill level of the workers, the more likely they are to benefit.

Exam tip

When a country gets richer overall, there is likely to be a bigger gap between rich and poor.

The opportunity cost to growth

In choosing to achieve economic growth, an economy has to give up other objectives. For example, a country could give more foreign aid, or improve the welfare of pensioners through more generous state aid. These transfer payments are not recorded as growth but may have greater value in terms of improved standards of living.

Evaluation: the opportunity cost of growth is hard to measure, as we cannot know what would have happened if another policy had been used.

Current and future living standards

With increased growth comes increased air and noise pollution, overcrowding, social dislocation and stress. Many people who are made richer by economic growth would say that they would love to return to the simpler life: they would not be happy though if you took away the money they had earned. On this basis, it is arguable how much economic growth improves some people's lives. See p. 68 on national happiness.

Now test yourself

TESTED

4 If economic growth makes someone in the UK's income rise so that she buys a new BMW car from Germany, what are the costs and benefits?

Answer on p. 112

Exam practice

1 The change in national income is measured at 0.4% in real terms for one year. This means that:
   A   Price levels are rising.
   B   There is a boom.
   C   The economy is in a recession.
   D   National income is rising slowly.   [1]
2 The growth rate in China is shown in Figure 9.4.

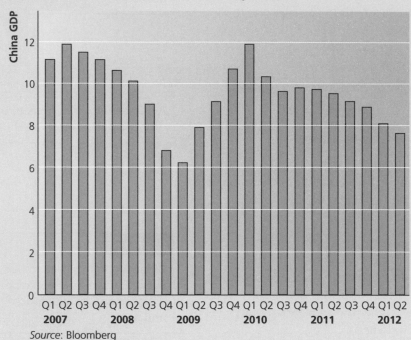

Source: Bloomberg

Figure 9.4 China GDP: quarter compared with previous quarter (annualised % figures)

   (a) Explain what was happening to the level of GDP in 2012.   [4]
   (b) Examine possible reasons for the change in the rate of growth rates.   [10]
   (c) Discuss the likely benefits of China's growth rate.   [20]

Answers and quick quizzes online

ONLINE

Summary

● There are two ways to measure growth: actual and potential.
● There are many causes of growth, and to analyse these we usually look at the forces acting on the components of aggregate demand: C + I + G + (X – M).
● The constraints on growth are many, and they depend on which country is being considered. The government might target the constraints on growth as a means of improving welfare in a country, for example by investing in new technological infrastructure.
● The benefits and costs of growth must be weighed against each other in your evaluation. Remember that while there may be benefits, there might be costs in both the short and long term that can cause more damage than the gains from increased income.

10 Macroeconomic objectives and policies

Possible macroeconomic objectives

The seven major objectives

REVISED

There are seven major macroeconomic objectives of governments across the world, but the priority given by each government varies, depending on its political slant. These seven objectives are:

1 Economic growth, i.e. an increase in real incomes or potential output.
2 A reduction in unemployment: the number of people available and willing to work but without employment should be ideally no more than 2%.
3 Control of inflation, i.e. preventing prices from rising too quickly.
4 Restoration of equilibrium in the balance of payments, meaning that there should not be either a persistent and heavy outflow or inflow of income and wealth.
5 Fiscal balance. Over time the government needs to pay its way, so taxation revenues must cover government spending over the course of the economic cycle.
6 Protection of the environment with its consequent impact on the various members of the global community.
7 Making the distribution of income more equal, i.e. ensuring that the top 10% slice (or decile) does not increase much faster than the bottom 10% slice.

Any policies adopted by governments in order to meet any one of these objectives is likely to have an impact on other objectives. Therefore, governments must choose which are its most important policies. Such decisions will determine the opportunity cost in terms of other policies or objectives.

Demand-side policies

There are two types of demand-side policy:
- **Monetary policy:** the manipulation of monetary variables in order to achieve government objectives.
- **Fiscal policy**: the manipulation of government spending and taxation in order to change aggregate demand

> **Demand-side policies** Any deliberate action taken by governments or monetary authorities to shift the aggregate demand curve.

Monetary policy instruments

REVISED

Monetary policy involves the setting of monetary variables, the most important of which are the interest rate (cost of credit or the reward for saving) and quantitative easing or QE (asset purchases to increase the money supply). Until 2008 the main instrument in most countries has been the interest rate.

Interest rates

If aggregate demand needs to decrease, the interest rate is raised. This means that C, I, and (X − M) will tend to fall. The AD shifts left. There are multiplier effects, increasing the impact of the change.

If aggregate demand needs to increase, the interest rate is cut. This means that C, I, and (X – M) will tend to rise. The AD shifts right. There are multiplier effects, increasing the impact of the change.

The interest rate is set by the Monetary Policy Committee (MPC) of the Bank of England, which meets every month to look at factors that will tend to make prices rise or fall over the coming 18 months or more. The committee takes a vote to determine the interest rate.

Asset purchases

After 2008, many monetary authorities found that interest rates alone could not stimulate aggregate demand. They therefore purchased long-term assets in the money or capital markets. As demand for these assets increased, the price of them rises, which in turn means the dividend yield on them falls. The amount of dividend relative to the price of the bond falls. This is the same impact as cutting interest rates, but has a direct effect on money markets. It means the bonds are more usable in the markets: because people want to buy them, the holders of bonds know they can be sold. It can mean money markets start working again, which is why quantitative easing (QE) is used in a credit crisis. The MPC in the UK spent £375 billion. The Federal Reserve in the US spent $3.7 trillion. From this we can see the USA policy response to the global financial crisis has been far greater than in the UK, and many argue that this is why the US economy recovered more quickly than the UK.

Fiscal policy instruments

REVISED

Fiscal policy can involve a government running a government budget or fiscal deficit, where government spending (G) is greater than the amount received in taxation (T). This has an expansionary effect on aggregate demand (AD), with multiplier effects. You can show this by shifting AD on a diagram, for example Figure 8.3 on p. 90.

Fiscal policy can involve a government running a government budget or fiscal surplus, where government spending (G) is less than the amount received in taxation (T). This has a contractionary effect on AD, with multiplier effects.

There are two types of tax: **direct** (on incomes) such as income tax and corporation tax, and **indirect** (on spending) such as VAT. When taxes are changed, the impact depends on which kind of tax is changed. A rise in direct taxes might mean people have reduced incentives to work hard and earn money, whilst if indirect taxes are raised, the cost of living increases, particularly for those on lower incomes because the tax paid will be a higher proportion of income than for those who do not spend all the money they earn.

Strengths of demand-side policies

REVISED

According to Keynesian economics:
- Demand-side policies are the only way to get a country out of demand-deficient unemployment and stagnation, at least in the short run.
- If the multiplier is large, they can have a significant impact on growth.
- If there is spare capacity, the economy can grow quickly.
- If used to control demand-pull inflation, they can act quickly and solve the problem.

Weaknesses of demand-side policies

According to classical economics:
- Expansionary demand-side policies only cause inflation in the long run.
- The multiplier might be so low that they have little effect.
- If there is no spare capacity, then supply-side policies are needed instead in order to achieve economic growth.
- The government can end up running a huge deficit, which adds to national debt, and this can become unsustainable (as in Greece from 2009 onwards).

Supply-side policies

These involve any attempt by the government to shift the aggregate supply (AS) curve to the right. The types of policies that may be used are as follows:
- Cutting corporation taxes (taxes on profits) so that firms have a strong incentive to produce more.
- Removing regulations and other restrictions that are preventing firms from growing, e.g. removing restrictions on mergers to allow these to take place.
- Encouraging investment by forcing banks to lend money, or by easing the credit situation (quantitative easing), or even just cutting the interest rate.
- Increasing competition in markets. Note that this might conflict with deregulation and allowing more monopolies (second point above).
- Privatising or subsidising industries, e.g. the Royal Mail.
- Improving the labour market by increasing educational standards.
- Productivity might increase by spending on the NHS. For example, if waiting lists are shorter, people can get back to work more promptly.
- Improved **incentives** for workers by cutting income tax rates and cutting benefits for out-of-work members of the labour force.
- Improving **infrastructure**, e.g. the transport system and internet coverage.
- Introducing measures to make imports cheaper, such as cutting tariffs, so that for many firms production costs fall. This is especially significant in the UK as the economy relies heavily on imported raw materials.

> An **incentive** is a factor that makes the labour resource more effective. It might be higher pay for working harder, or more profits if businesses are run successfully.
>
> **Infrastructure** is the capital assets that enable resources to move and be moved, for example motorways and internet connections.

> **Exam tip**
>
> Note that cutting interest rates can lead to increases in AD and AS.

Now test yourself

1 Why do economists use deciles and quintiles?

Answer on p. 112

Conflicts and trade-offs between objectives and policies

Conflicts between objectives

There are many possible conflicts between the seven objectives listed above. Below is a selection of commonly observed **trade-offs**.

> **Exam tip**
>
> Be careful not to confuse conflicts between objectives, e.g. inflation and growth, with conflicts between policies, e.g. fiscal expansion and monetary contraction.

> A **trade-off** occurs when one objective is achieved at the expense of another.

Conflict 1: inflation and unemployment

When the government tries to control inflation it is likely to try to dampen aggregate demand.

- Less spending will mean less upward pressure on prices.
- The government might increase taxes or the Monetary Policy Committee (MPC) might increase interest rates.
- The impact of these may prevent inflation but they will also mean less spending in the economy.
- Firms may start laying off workers because they are unable to sell all their goods and services, and as workers are laid off incomes fall and so the cycle continues.
- So, there appears to be a trade-off between the objective of controlling inflation and unemployment because in trying to control inflation, unemployment will rise.

This works in the other direction as well. Here is an example:

- If the government is trying to control unemployment it might start spending more on training workers or subsidising firms to take on more workers.
- This increased spending in the economy is likely to make prices in general rise.
- This is because there is more money chasing the same amount of goods and services.

The trade-off between inflation and unemployment is illustrated in the Phillips curve as shown in Figure 10.1. At point A there is high inflation and low unemployment, but if the government tries to move to point B it only gets rid of inflation at the expense of unemployment.

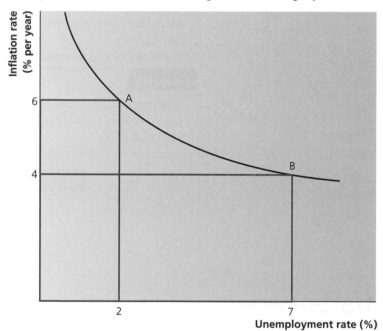

Figure 10.1 The Phillips curve

Now test yourself

2 What does the Phillips curve show?

Answer on p. 112

Conflict 2: economic growth and sustainability

When an economy grows, standards of living tend to improve.

- For standards of living to be sustainable, growth must not occur at the expense of future generations.
- There is a conflict between enjoying a resource today and someone else enjoying it in the future.
- This is most important when considering those affected by damage to the environment when we consume resources today.
- So, if our increased use of fuels means that there is more global warming, growth may not be as desirable as it first appears.
- Governments must make a choice, weighing up the welfare of today's generation with that of tomorrow to achieve **sustainable growth**.

> **Sustainable growth** is growth that does not compromise the welfare of future generations.

Conflict 3: inflation and equilibrium on the current account of the balance of payments

Controlling inflation should make a country more competitive internationally and therefore lead to an improvement on the balance of payments.

- Exports become relatively cheap and imports relatively expensive.
- Therefore, controlling inflation should not conflict with dealing with a balance of payments deficit.
- However, the actions required to control inflation can damage the balance of payments. For example, raising interest rates to control inflation might have the effect of raising the exchange rate which in turn makes exports expensive and imports cheap.
- By contrast, contractionary fiscal policy — which might alternatively be used to control inflation — tends to improve the balance of payments because people have less money to purchase foreign goods.

> **Typical mistake**
>
> Confusing the budget with the balance of payments. A budget refers to the government's fiscal position and that the balance of payments is a record of international flows of funds.

TESTED ☐

Now test yourself

3 What is contractionary fiscal policy?

Answer on p. 112

Conflicts between macroeconomic policies

REVISED ☐

Conflict 1: fiscal policy and monetary policy

Changes in the planned levels of spending and taxation by the government (fiscal policy) have a direct impact on the decision making of the MPC (monetary policy).

- If the MPC believes that fiscal policy is too loose, e.g. government spending is too generous relative to taxation, then the MPC might seek to counterbalance the effect on inflation by raising interest rates.
- If the MPC believes that fiscal policy is too tight, e.g. government spending is not generous relative to taxation, then the MPC might seek to counterbalance the effect on inflation by cutting interest rates.

When fiscal policy means that there is an enormous deficit, this has to be paid for by borrowing. Increased demands in the money markets for funds means that other borrowers, apart from the government, might have to pay more to borrow money. So financing fiscal policy can have an impact on market interest rates.

Now test yourself

TESTED

4 Why does loose fiscal policy affect interest rates?

Answer on p. 112

Conflict 2: monetary policy and supply-side policy

Changes in interest rates and other monetary policy decisions have a direct impact on the costs of firms, therefore shifting the aggregate supply curve.

● If interest rates rise, it will costs firms more to produce, which might mean that firms are willing to produce less at any particular price level.
● If interest rates fall, it will costs firms less to produce, which might mean that firms are willing to produce more at any particular price level.

> **Exam tip**
>
> Monetary policy is not intended to influence the supply-side of the economy, but this is an impact the MPC must take into account when making its interest rate decisions.

Now test yourself

TESTED

5 Why do firms borrow money?

Answer on p. 112

Conflict 3: supply-side policy and fiscal policy

Changes in most supply-side policies will have a direct impact on government spending, i.e. fiscal policy. For example:

● Improving education and health services to encourage people to be more productive requires high levels of government spending.
● Increasing the length of education also means that governments will not receive money via taxes from income those students might have earned had they been at work.

In most cases:

● Supply-side policies tend to *increase* the budget deficit in the short term.
● Supply-side policies can *decrease* the budget deficit in the long term, as improved human capital means higher incomes that can be taxed by the government.

However, some supply-side policies, such as reducing bureaucracy, are unlikely to make a significant impact upon government spending and taxation (G and T).

Some supply-side policies, such as privatisation and cutting benefits, will tend to *reduce* the budget deficit. Privatisation is a one-off fiscal improvement, and cutting benefits could increase long-term costs to the government because of the social problems involved.

> **Typical mistake**
>
> Never assume that all supply-side policies work. Many policies take years to achieve, and some might not achieve success at all. The current changes in the education system might be seen as attempt to improve the supply-side of the economy, but if, for example, some young people become alienated by the new exam system then you could argue that the supply-side policy shifts the aggregate supply curve to the left.

Now test yourself

TESTED

6 Why does a cut in bureaucracy improve the supply-side with no impact on the fiscal position?
7 Why do supply-side policies tend to improve human capital?

Answers on p. 112

Exam practice answers and quick quizzes at **www.hoddereducation.co.uk/myrevisionnotes**

Typical mistake

Try to avoid being 'one-sided', for example when assessing supply-side policies such as cutting benefits. Remember that there are two sides to every issue and, if you want to earn evaluation marks, you must weigh up both sides of the argument. Evaluation is worth up to 25% of the marks in Paper 2.

Exam practice

1 Explain the likely impact of a rise in the base rate of interest on the distribution of income. [2]
2 Explain the term indirect tax. Give an example in your answer. [2]
3 Which of the following is correct? If everything else is unchanged, a rise in indirect tax is most likely to cause:
  A aggregate demand to shift to the left and aggregate supply left/decrease
  B aggregate demand to shift to the right and aggregate supply left/decrease
  C aggregate demand to shift to the left and aggregate supply right/increase
  D aggregate demand to shift to the right and aggregate supply right/increase [1]
4 Using an appropriate diagram, explain what is meant by the term 'supply-side policies'. [6]
5 Discuss the use of supply-side policies as a means of addressing a problem of rising youth unemployment. [15]
6 Evaluate whether demand-side policies will be successful in reducing unemployment. [20]
7 Evaluate the likely impact of a rise in the base rate of interest on at least **two** government objectives. [20]

Answers and quick quizzes online

ONLINE

Summary

- No objective can be achieved by governments without some form of impact on other objectives. There are seven major economic objectives of governments involving control of:
  1 growth
  2 employment
  3 inflation
  4 balance of payments
  5 fiscal balance
  6 environmental sustainability
  7 distribution of income
- Some of these objectives are possible to achieve together, but for some there is a trade-off, i.e. more of one means less of another. You will need to be able to reason

through the relationship between at least two of these seven objectives.
- When a macroeconomic policy is applied, there will be direct effects, which may or may not be seen as a successful outcome, and indirect effects, which may or may not be beneficial.
- The government has to prioritise the objectives that it believes are the most important at any one time, and the economist will try to predict how effective these priorities will be and what the effects of implementation will be on a wide range of variables. No economic policy comes without costs, in addition to knowing what the main macroeconomic policies are (monetary and fiscal) you also need to know the possible side effects.

Now test yourself answers

Chapter 1

1. b, c and e are positive statements because these can be verified by reference to data.

   a and d are normative statements because they are subjective and based on value judgements.

2. (a) Land because copper is a natural resource which is included in the economic definition of land.

   (b) Enterprise because the woman has taken the risks to start a business.

   (c) Capital because the robots are used to make other goods.

   (d) Labour because the person is working for a business to makes goods and services.

3. (a) Capital good.

   (b) Consumer good.

   (c) Consumer good/service.

   (d) Capital good.

4. Resources are scarce but wants are infinite, so choices must be made.

5. The holiday in Greece — this is the real cost of making a choice.

6. No resources are sacrificed in their use, so the opportunity cost is zero.

7.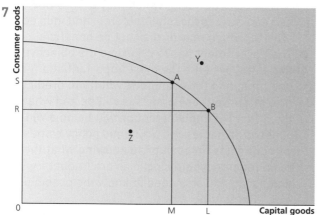

   (a) At Z there will be unemployed resources because this point is not on the PPF.

   (b) Point Y is currently unattainable. It could only be achieved if there was an outward shift in the PPF.

   (c) LM capital goods.

   (d) (i) Increasing the current output of consumer goods would increase current living standards.

   (ii) However, future living standards may fall because fewer capital goods are being produced.

8. (a) An outward (rightward) shift because productivity would increase the productive capacity of the country.

   (b) An inward shift on the PPF because productive capacity would have decreased.

   (c) This would cause an outward shift in the PPF because the extra capital would enable output per worker to increase.

   (d) This represents an increase in the working population causing an increase in the productive capacity of the country. Therefore, the PPF would shift outwards.

9. d: The demand for specialist products makes it very difficult to increase specialisation. Specialisation is best suited to the production of mass-produced goods, which enables the job to be broken down into small tasks.

10. Money enables a person to work in a highly specialist job. The money he/she is paid in can then be used to buy other goods and services.

11. ● private ownership of resources

    ● profit motive

    ● competition between firms

    ● prices determined by the forces of supply and demand

12. Consumer sovereignty is the power of consumers to determine what is produced by their preferences. Firms respond to consumer demand by producing the goods and services which consumers buy.

13. ● freedom to own resources

    ● efficiency associated with the profit motive and competition

    ● higher rates of growth than in command economies

14. There is freedom to own resources; those who own resources are likely to earn more income than those who do not own resources.

15. Any three of:

    ● Danger that there will be unemployed resources.

    ● The free market economy is likely to be subject to booms and slumps associated with the trade cycle.

    ● No account is taken of external costs and benefits.

    ● Danger that monopolies will occur.

16. The state.

17 ● The state can ensure all workers are employed.
   ● There is likely to be greater equality.
18 There is no profit motive and no competition.

Chapter 2

1 (a) The amount demanded at given prices over a certain period of time.
  (b) (i) a rightward shift in the demand curve
      (ii) a leftward shift in the demand curve
      (iii) a rightward shift in the demand curve for houses because the substitute, rented accommodation, has increased in price
      (iv) a leftward shift in the demand curve because it has become more expensive to buy a house

2 (a) PED = % change in quantity demanded/% change in price

$$= \frac{-10\%}{20\%} = -0.5$$

This implies that demand is price inelastic since the result is between 0 and −1.

  (b) PED $= \frac{-15\%}{10\%} = -1.5$

This implies that demand is price elastic.

  (c) PED $= \frac{6\%}{-6\%} = -1$.

This implies that demand is unitary elastic.

3 Total revenue will increase because the price will have risen by a larger percentage than the fall in quantity demanded.

4 Demand is price elastic because the rise in price must have caused a more than proportionate fall in quantity demanded.

5 Demand is unitary elastic because the increase in price must have caused an exactly proportionate fall in the quantity demanded.

6 There are many substitutes.

7 Inelastic because for many people there are no effective substitutes and coffee forms part of their daily diet.

8 Milk is a non-durable product and part of the everyday diet of many consumers.

9 (a) (i) +15% ÷ +10% = +1.5. Therefore, tea and coffee are substitutes since the result is positive.
      (ii) −10% ÷ +5% = −2. Therefore, X and Y are complements because the result is negative.
  (b) C

10 (a) −9% ÷ −3% = + 3. This implies that new cars are a normal good (the result is positive) and that demand is income elastic (the fall in income has led to a more than proportionate decrease in demand).
  (b) −2% ÷ +5% = −0.4. Therefore, soya is an inferior good because the result is negative.
  (c) +2% ÷ +10% = +0.2. Therefore, demand for oranges is income inelastic (the result is between 0 and +1).

11 The amount producers are willing to offer for sale at given prices in a particular period of time.

12 (a) Rightward shift of the supply curve because a subsidy reduces production costs.
  (b) Leftward shift of the supply curve because higher wages would increase production costs.
  (c) Rightward shift of the supply curve because output per worker has risen.
  (d) Leftward shift of the supply curve because less tea will be available.

13 (a) 2% ÷ 20% = 0.1. Therefore, supply is inelastic since the result is between 0 and 1.
  (b) 15% ÷ 5% = 3. Therefore, supply is elastic since the result is greater than +1.

14 Supply would be inelastic because tomatoes are perishable and cannot be stored, and there is a long growing period.

15 It is possible that the supply of butter would be elastic if there were stocks available in refrigerated warehouses.

16 Excess supply because the quantity supplied will be greater than the quantity demanded.

17 Market forces would cause an extension of demand and a contraction in the quantity supplied.

18 (a) The supply curve will shift to the left causing a rise in the price of beef and a fall in quantity.
  (b) The demand curve will shift to the right causing a rise in price and a rise in the quantity.
  (c) The supply curve will shift to the right causing a fall in price and an increase in quantity.
  (d) The demand curve will shift to the left causing the price and quantity to fall.

19 The supply curve would shift to the left and become steeper.

Chapter 3

1 A market is said to fail if resources are not allocated in the most efficient way possible.

2 Externalities; public goods; information gaps.

3 The social marginal cost must be equal to the social marginal benefit.

4 Private costs: raw materials, wages; cost of fertiliser to the farmer.

External costs: waste discharge into river; loss of income to fishermen because these are fewer fish.

5 Private benefits: extra salary from gaining a degree; job satisfaction.

External benefits: increased economic growth; higher productivity of workers meaning goods are more competitive internationally.

6 Private goods are excludable, i.e. it is possible to prevent everyone from consuming the product and rivalrous — consumption by one person means that less is available for others.

7 Because it is impossible to exclude people from consuming the product.

8 By the use of detectors vans and hand-held detectors to ensure that those using televisions have a licence.

9 A dentist will usually have much greater knowledge and information about a person's teeth and dental hygiene than the patient. Consequently, it is possible that a patient may be given unnecessary treatment, e.g. a filling.

Chapter 4

1 It implies that the producer has to bear the cost of the pollution, so the negative externality is internalised by the producer causing it.

2 It may be difficult to (i) determine the extent of the external costs and (ii) to place a monetary value on the external costs caused in the production process.

3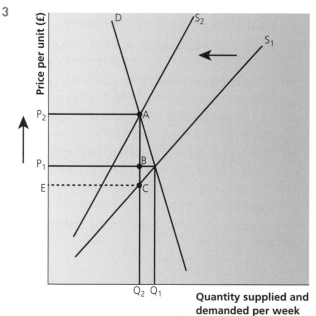

(a) Tax borne by consumer: P_1P_2AB
(b) Tax borne by producer: EP_1BC

4 This would cause the supply curve for those involved in electricity generation from wind farms to shift to the left. Consequently, there would be an increase in price and decrease in output.

5 To provide an incentive for farmers to increase production of wheat. Farmers would now know

how much they would receive for the production of each kilo of wheat.

6 The quantity demanded by consumers would decrease because the price would be higher than the free market price. The quantity supplied would increase because the farmers would be encouraged to produce more as the price would be higher than the free market price.

7 The government can issue permits to pollute up to a certain limit. Those companies using clean technology can sell them to those using dirty technology. Over time, the number of these permits could be reduced forcing up their price so providing a growing incentive for firms to invest in new technology.

8 It may be very difficult and expensive to enforce laws and regulations designed to reduce pollution. Further, finding proof that a firm is responsible for pollution might not be possible without sufficient evidence.

9 Further away from the socially efficient output.

10 If the fishing quotas allow too many fish to be caught then it is possible that stocks will diminish and ultimately there may be no fish left.

Chapter 5

1 A recession means that incomes are falling, output is falling and spending is falling. The characteristics tend to be lower living standards, increasing unemployment, and many firms going out of business. From the government's point of view there tends to be more spending (on benefits) and reduced tax receipts.

2 It may mean that it could enjoy higher living standards, but this is not guaranteed. It might mean that people are working longer hours or live in much more crowded cities, for example.

3 Happiness takes into account the quality of life rather than the income alone. It is difficult to collect accurate data, but a picture can be built up over time of changes in happiness, and the ONS attempts to do this in its official statistics. Government policy can have a significant impact on happiness, for example by spending money on facilities for disabled people or providing efficient library services. However, some people think that the provision of these services is not the role of the government, and therefore policy should be focused on increased incomes for all, which will have indirect effects on other services as government revenues will increase as the economy grows.

4 No. If it is a one-off spike when prices go up sharply (and usually come down again) then it is neither general nor sustained. However, it could be a *cause* of inflation because when oil prices go up the cost of production rises for most firms, and this is likely to cause firms in general to raise their prices.

5 Similar items can be bought in high- and low-cost shops, so a selection of prices is gathered for each item. There are about 18 000 separate price quotations used every month in compiling the indices, covering nearly 700 representative consumer goods and services. Prices are collected in about 150 areas.

6 High rates of inflation have impacts on other macro objectives of governments: to some extent they can worsen the distribution of income (people on low fixed incomes such as pensioners will see real wages fall), but a high rate of inflation can also narrow the distribution of income (real values of savings and debts decrease), so if those with high incomes have high savings and those with low incomes have more debts, the distribution of income will widen. International trade suffers if a country has higher inflation than its trading partners (exports become relatively expensive and imports relatively cheap) and there are adverse effects if interest rates rise to fight inflation because this often leads to an increase in the value of the currency.

7 Reasons might include: housing costs are excluded such as mortgage interest repayments and rent. The 650 items in the 'basket' are changed only once a year, but tastes and fashions change more quickly than this and 'special offers' temporarily change people's spending habits. For people with atypical spending patterns, such as vegetarians and non-drivers, the CPI will be unrepresentative. Quality and technology of goods change over time and this is difficult to incorporate in the measurement of CPI. For example, the quality of instant cameras has dramatically improved on a monthly basis and the basket of goods is not changed often enough to reflect this.

8 It falls by 3%.

9 It represents the people of working age who are economically inactive, e.g. students or those caring for dependants.

10 There are strict criteria for claiming JSA and many are not eligible. For example if you refuse work that you have been offered, have a high level of savings or have a spouse with a high income you may not be eligible.

11 The claimant count records people who receive a financial reward for declaring themselves unemployed, whereas in the ILO method there is no reward for saying that you are unemployed. So when times are hard and there is not much money around in the economy (in a recession) the JSA tends to rise relative to the ILO. People have a stronger incentive to claim the JSA payments,

are less likely to have high levels of savings or spouses with high incomes etc., which might have made them ineligible.

12 Because full-time students are not included in the official figures for employment or unemployment neither should change. However, many students do some paid work (EU students do not have any restrictions within the EU) so the level of employment might rise as casual vacancies are filled.

13 It is an import because money is flowing out of the country. Most people get confused with this because they think of themselves leaving the country as an exit not an entry. Remember to think about money flows, not the physical movement of goods or people.

Chapter 6

1 A movement along the AD curve happens when there is a change in the price level. This might be because all costs have risen, i.e. a shift in aggregate supply. A movement in AD occurs when one of the determinants of aggregate demand changes. For example, an increase in investment will increase AD. In this case, there is a **decrease in government spending (G)** so aggregate demand decreases (shifts to the left).

2 Consumption will rise.

3 Initially there might be a decrease in aggregate demand as the price elasticity of demand for imports and exports tends to be low, but as time goes by you would expect aggregate demand to increase. People abroad start buying the cheaper exports and people at home stop buying the expensive imports.

Chapter 7

1 This is the Keynesian method of drawing the AS curve. It illustrates that there can be equilibrium price level and real national output even when there is unemployment or spare capacity in the economy.

2 Interest rate increases will make loans more expensive for firms, so an increase is likely to make aggregate supply fall.

Chapter 8

1 It will rise more slowly. Government spending is an injection into the circular flow of income, so a fall in the injection means that incomes will rise less quickly than they did.

2 Equilibrium means there is a balance, and no tendency to change. It should mean that there are no surpluses or deficits, and markets are clearing. However, according to Keynes, equilibrium can occur while there is demand-deficient unemployment.

3 £2 million (2 × £1 million).

Chapter 9

1 You would expect a rise in both AD and AS. So growth rises.

2 The level of GDP has risen by 2%, whereas in the past it had risen more quickly at 3.2%. GDP has certainly not fallen even if growth rates fall.

3 High exchange rates make the price of exports expensive in foreign countries, so this may stop people buying them. If exports fall, AD falls because X is a component of AD and there are multiplier effects. Likewise, if exchange rates are high, imports are cheap and so if imports are increased, then because this is a negative component of AD, then AD falls with multiplier effects. However, a high exchange rate can have the reverse effect if the price elasticity of demand for exports and imports is low.

4 The increased import will worsen the balance of payments. If the car uses a lot of fuel, there will be increased carbon emissions, and the fuel itself will be an import.

Chapter 10

1 Deciles (10% slices of data) and quintiles (20% slices of data) help us to compare chunks of data

rather than the extremes. For example, it is a more helpful measure of inequality if we are not too swayed by the extremely poor and extremely rich, as these make the results unrepresentative of most people.

2 The Phillips curve illustrates a negative relationship between inflation (on the vertical axis) and unemployment. The implication is that if you are prepared to forgo one you can achieve success in controlling the other.

3 Contractionary fiscal policy is when government spending and taxation is used to dampen demand, perhaps by cutting government spending or raising taxation.

4 Because deficits have to be financed by borrowing. Increased demand for loanable funds puts up interest rates.

5 Firms need to pay for resources which they then transform into goods and services that they can then sell. The time taken to transfer the resources into receipts for payment means that firms need to borrow.

6 Less bureaucracy means there are fewer rules and regulations for firms when they operate in a country. For example, it might mean that firms can take on more workers without doing full checks on their criminal records. This will cut costs for firms and mean they can increase output at a lower cost that it would otherwise be, but there are no direct payments as a result — except that those workers will start paying tax on their incomes more quickly.

7 Investment in people, such as spending on health or education, improves the productive potential of the workforce. Human assets are worth more to the economy.